Working with Water

by Jeremy Evans

Neilson

© Jeremy Evans 2009
First Published 2009
The Royal Yachting Association
RYA House, Ensign Way, Hamble
Southampton SO31 4YA
Tel: 0845 345 0400
Fax: 0845 345 0329
E-mail: publications@rya .org.uk
Web: www.rya.org.uk
ISBN: 978-1905-104-819
RYA Order Code: G65

Totally Chlorine Free **Sustainable Forests**

A CIP record of this book is available from the British Library.

Note: While all reasonable care had been taken in the preparation of this book, the publisher takes no responsibility for the use of the methods or products or contracts described in the book.

Cover Design: Pete Galvin
Typesetting and Design: Kevin Slater
Proofreading and indexing: Alan Thatcher
Printed in China through World Print

FOREWORD

I am well aware how fortunate that in the course of my career I have spent a great deal of time out on the water. Boats and the sea have always been my passion. To be able to translate that to the workplace has always been a source of great pleasure to me.

Back in the dark ages when I first started hunting for a job, the marine industry was not the multi-million pound industry it is today, and getting a job in this line of work was something of a struggle, so I was fortunate to get involved. These days, there is an absolute plethora of opportunities within the industry, and it, is more of a case of working out what you want to do and how to get involved.

This is where Working on Water comes to the fore, and it is an invaluable guide; providing you with a really useful overview. Have a read and, who knows, it may change your life. At the very least it could change your career.

Rod Carr OBE

WORKING WITH WATER

Do you want to work with sailing or power boats? The opportunities are excellent, since the recreational boating industry has snowballed over the past few decades, providing a tremendous range of work for almost all ages and abilities. This means you can not only do something that you really enjoy, but also get paid for it. Salaries may be (a lot) lower than a conventional profession, but the work could not be more rewarding.

Most working opportunities in sailing and powerboating have become closely linked to RYA training and qualifications. For instance, a young teenager who volunteers as an Assistant Instructor can progress to paid work as a Dinghy or Windsurfing Instructor from the age of 16. That opens the gates to a wonderful choice of holidays or gap year jobs, both at home and abroad, which in time could lead to joining the lead boat crew on a flotilla or working your way up with the management team.

Working as a yacht or powerboat instructor requires a high level of qualifications, while working on superyachts provides a glamorous alternative that can lead to a highly paid job, either as a short term or full time career. And if you like the idea of working in a glamorous part of the industry, how about becoming a professional racing crew or Olympic sailor? Such elite jobs are not widely available, but the prospects for an exciting and possibly well-paid lifestyle are exceptional. Expert coaches are required to provide tuition and support for racers at all levels and this service can also be turned into a part time or full time career. Other options may include working as a shore-based instructor of RYA courses, or entering the profession with ambitions for a full time career in designing, marketing or building boats.

The opportunities available for people who wish to work on water are fascinating and wide ranging. This book is a guide to basic career paths, backed up by the personal experience of people who have experienced a wide range of jobs in the quest for a working lifestyle that is rewarding, in every sense of the word.

Jeremy Evans

Minorca Sailing

RYA Instructors work around the world

During 2008 over 18,000 RYA qualified instructors worked at over 2,000 RYA recognised training centres in more than 20 countries around the world.

"Look, no hands!" Teaching sailing is a great way to work through a summer, with potential for a full time watersports career.

Flying Fish

CONTENTS

Jeremy Evans

MIND THE GAP

FITTING WORK IN WITH SCHOOL AND UNIVERSITY

1

If you love sailing or windsurfing, there are plenty of opportunities to fill your summer holiday, have a great time and even end up a little richer than when you started. Working as a yacht instructor, teaching RYA Day Skipper courses in the Canary Islands, could be part of a gap year or full time career.

INSTRUCTORS IN DEMAND

There is always big demand for seasonal dinghy and windsurfing instructors and you will get paid – not much, but enough to have fun. Qualified instructors should theoretically earn more than unqualified staff, but prior experience is more highly valued. The employer should provide flights and transfers, for which they require commitment that you will stay for a minimum length of time. Some will charge for your 'uniform' – mostly T-shirt and shorts – or ask for a deposit as part of this commitment.

Accommodation should be provided, but don't expect to live like the clients. 'Workers' may have to put up with a basic and crowded environment, which is not enhanced if fellow workers enjoy living in squalor! It's worth being forceful on issues such as cleaning and washing up – concepts that some people new to the outside world may find incomprehensible. If you're lucky, the deal may include all or

Time off can be used to pursue your own passions.

some of your food which will otherwise be the major weekly expense that drains your money. Whereabouts you work will also affect how much you spend. If you're teaching sailing in the backwoods with no bars, clubs or other expensive distractions, you will certainly end up better off but possibly get very bored.

IT'S NOT YOUR HOLIDAY

Teaching sailing at a Mediterranean style centre is not a 'holiday'. You should expect plenty of fun and a great experience, while being worked hard. Most instructors have to work long hours and can expect one day off a week at best. It may be unpleasantly hot, rigging or derigging boats gets extremely repetitive, you must always be nice to customers regardless of the situation. Some instructors find this very hard, can't stand the pace and have to be sent

An instructor is essentially a teacher.

Dealing with all kinds of people is a major part of the job.

home. But if you can cope, the perks of the job should include time to enjoy your own sailing on their equipment, either during time off or when customers have finished for the day.

Keen sailors who want to work as instructors should check the level of equipment at different centres, which may range from basic and boring to true high performance kit. It's also important to check out average wind conditions, so you are not disappointed if winds are invariably light.

Many gap year students who work abroad appear to find it a great lifestyle, since they return year after year to work in the same places during the high season summer vacation. If all goes well you're in a pleasant location, enjoy beautiful weather, get time to sail or windsurf with someone else's equipment, have fun and make lots of new friends. There should be a good feeling of camaraderie between instructors and all other staff, with everyone in the same situation, but you should also expect the normal ups and downs created by friction and relationships.

For some gap year students, the disadvantage of Mediterranean style centres is that low wages make it difficult to save any money at all. If that's what you want, consider working at a UK sailing school where they pay considerably more to attract seasonal staff. You could earn more than twice as much as abroad – perhaps £250 a week for working maximum possible hours – but if no accommodation is provided, the increased cost of living and travelling to work may cancel out any advantage. On the plus side, you won't be living on top of the job and can enjoy a break from the clients.

GET THE RIGHT CERTIFICATES

Working for a British company – in the UK or abroad – a suitable RYA certificate will almost certainly be required to show you are qualified to teach. (A few people who teach at Mediterranean style centres may not have this valuable piece of paper, but rely on very good connections to get the job.)

Teaching dinghy sailing is the most popular gap year summer season job and is widely available for those who successfully complete a five day RYA Dinghy Instructor course. Before starting, you must attend a pre-assessment of sailing ability which might include unusual skills such as sailing backwards and rudderless. At the end of the course you may be given a clear pass, or be required to get more experience as an assistant instructor before your RYA instructor's log book is fully signed off. By the time you've paid for all the necessary extras – pre-assessment plus First Aid and Level 2

Powerboat certificates – the cost of a dinghy instructor certificate could be at least £500, after which you can start earning by working.

The biggest demand for seasonal sailing instructors is during the summer holidays, which is perfect timing for the start of a gap year. When the schools go back in September less instructors are required, but this is balanced by many instructors leaving for university, with the result that more instructors are hired for the autumn. The Mediterranean season closes at the end of October and does not open again until April. The situation in the UK is similar, with school parties and other groups providing potential work through both spring and autumn, but not in the winter when demand for dinghy instructors is virtually extinct unless you can work where the sun still shines brightly – perhaps in Australia or the Caribbean where you can also find RYA recognised centres.

Be prepared to jump in and help your students, as demonstrated by this instructor at Cobnor Activities Centre.

THE CARIBBEAN CONNECTION

Some gap year students work at ski resorts through the winter season, the end of which coincides neatly with the start of the sailing season. Best advice for those who want to keep working with sailing may be to join the annual yacht exodus to the Caribbean. This starts in early autumn, when the Mediterranean charter season comes to an end and yachts head across the Atlantic for Antigua, St Lucia, Barbados and all those islands with lovely names. First problem. How do you get a passage? The most direct method is to stalk marinas where the biggest yachts are located, with Antibes on the French Riviera or Palma in Majorca among the top choices. If you've got the nerve, you can go round every yacht asking if they need crew.

Signing on with a www crew agency is a less challenging option. Be warned that they only bring together skippers seeking crews and crews seeking yachts, which does not guarantee you will get a 'quality ride'. The problem is that once you're on a yacht, it may be very difficult to get off. I met a couple of gap year students whose rocky experience is not untypical. They signed on with a well known crew agency and were immediately offered a ride as unpaid crew down to the Canaries. Maybe a 30 foot yacht was a bit on the small side, but dates were perfect to fit in with the start of the ARC (Atlantic Rally for Cruisers), which is an annual migration from Las Palmas to St Lucia. It did not take them long to realise they had signed on with the owner/skipper from hell, who was incompetent with dubious sailing ability on a yacht in a very poor state of repair. After a grim trip across the Bay of Biscay, the boys were greatly relieved to jump ship in the north of Spain, after which they had to pay their own travel back to the UK.

Sunsail

A good place to be in winter…

Enjoy the good life with a winter season working in the Caribbean. Local authorities on the islands can be very hot on work permits, making it easier for visitors to work afloat than on shore.

On their return, the crew agency came up with a much better proposition. How about a ride across the Atlantic on a stylish 45 foot cruiser-racer with all carbon trimmings which was being collected by its new American owner. They appeared to blow that opportunity when the owner asked, "Do you drink?" during a phone interview. "Ha, ha, ha!" they replied, "We can drink anyone under the table!" The American owner did not share or understand their sense of humour and there was no invitation to join his boat. They resorted to grovelling on bended knees, eventually persuading him that they really could manage to sail without alcohol. So far as I know the trip went well.

Once you've arrived in the Caribbean, local work permits may pose a hurdle on the islands. However work on large charter yachts can be available if you are in the right place at the right time and have the right face for the job. Falmouth Harbour in Antigua is rated as one of the best places to find a job as deck hand or stewardess. Be aware that sexism, ageism and racism are factors you may need to contend with. Advantages of working as crew include the opportunity to sail on a beautiful boat and save most of your wages, since accommodation and food are provided. Disadvantages revolve around a 'below stairs' lifestyle in which crew and clients lead separate lives. While it's luxury for the clients, crew live in crammed quarters in the forepeak and are expected to become 'invisible' when not required to sail the boat or serve food and drinks.

How about a ride across the Atlantic on a stylish 45 foot cruiser-racer with all carbon trimmings…

SCRUBBERS OR SKIPPERS

The pecking order among crew may be decided by plain seniority or who is sleeping with whom, with the skipper at the top of the pay roll on a going rate of $1,000 a foot per annum which is greatly enhanced by tips at the end of each charter. At the other end of the scale, day workers get $12-$15 per hour regardless of age or experience, but beware that their work often involves cleaning boats to a bizarre level. Everything on a top charter yacht must be scrubbed and polished to never ending perfection, including such tasks as washing the mast from top to bottom or cleaning the shrouds inch by inch with a toothbrush.

Sex, drugs and too much alcohol are the normal things to watch out for if you pursue working on a yacht. However, old hands insist that it's most important to avoid getting on a 'problem' boat where the crew are at each another's throats or a difficult skipper makes life miserable. The best advice is to judge the boat and its crew with gut feeling from first impressions – never jump at the first offer of a job regardless.

One problem is that although there is lots of daywork available in the Caribbean, many charter boats want a commitment of a year which makes a permanent on-board job more difficult to find. However it's cheap to live, so two or three days of work a week should be enough if you are not overly extravagant. It's altogether a very different experience from working at a dinghy sailing centre where you have a manager, regular routine and know what you'll be paid each week, but the more independent lifestyle is great practice for university!

ON THE BEACH

A typical beach club employs a large number of staff with a wide range of skills:

■ On the waterfront – Beach manager in charge of dinghies and windsurfers, working with dinghy and windsurfing instructors and kids' sailing instructors. Other watersports instructors might be required to teach canoeing, kitesurfing, waterskiing and wakeboarding.

■ Yachting – Yacht instructors to take out clients and a base engineer to care for the boats.

■ Flotilla – Skipper, host and engineer.

■ Activities & Fitness – Instructors and leaders, providing skills ranging from yoga to mountain biking.

■ Childcare – Manager, activity leaders and nannies.

■ Hospitality – Reception and front of house staff whose work will include meeting and greeting clients, as well as ensuring they have a wonderful holiday.

Getting paid to windsurf in the sun is enough to make anyone smile. Just remember that when you're working, it's not your holiday.

Flying Fish

CHECKLIST WHEN WORKING ABROAD

Salary
- Is payment in local currency or sterling?
- Do you have to pay any taxes?
- What will you have to pay for? Is free accommodation provided? Do you get free meals? Do you get a discount on drinks at the club bar?

Bonus When a satisfactory season is completed, many companies pay a bonus which can provide a welcome boost to low wages. Beware that you may lose the bonus if you leave the job early.

Holiday Everyone needs a break. It's not unknown for small companies to work instructors 7/7, but the majority should guarantee at least one day off a week. Some are generous enough to provide a paid week's holiday for employees who have worked a sufficent number of weeks during the summer season.

Accommodation If you work abroad, accommodation should normally be provided. Check how many people are expected to share a room, as well as cooking facilities and showers.

Travel Flight and transfer costs should be covered from the UK to your overseas resort and back at the end of your contract. You may be able to claim travel expenses to your UK departure airport. Check what happens if something goes wrong. Will your employer pay for the flight home?

Are you covered? Some companies provide insurance cover for emergency medical and dental expenses. The addition of cover for personal belongings will be a bonus.

Training The employer should ensure that you are properly trained in all aspects of your new job. In some circumstances, you may be able to gain RYA qualifications at no cost.

What will you wear? Many employers will require you to wear their uniform when on duty. Some will ask you to pay for it as well! The theory is that you will then take proper care of your gear.

What are the perks?
- Apart from working on the water in a holiday location, a major perk of the job is likely to be free use of equipment in your free time, though clients will always have first choice.
- If you are looking to fill out a gap year, consider working for a company which also runs ski holidays, providing the opportunity for up to four months of winter work.

SAILING
WORKING AS A DINGHY OR CATSAILING INSTRUCTOR

Getting qualified as a dinghy or cat instructor opens up plenty of job opportunities, both in the UK and abroad. Three leading centres, based in the Mediterranean and Britain, provide an insight into work that can be very enjoyable for those who are prepared to sign up to high standards.

Jeremy Evans

WILDWIND – VASSILIKI, GREECE

Wildwind

Simon Morgan is the founder, owner and managing director of Wildwind, the top high wind sailing centre at Vassiliki on the island of Levkas. A typical day is divided between light winds for learning in the mornings, followed by Force 5 blasting in the afternoons when many clients favour catsailing.

Simon, how many instructors and other staff do Wildwind employ during the high and low season?

We have twelve beach staff for the low season, increasing to twenty for the high season, plus three on the 'Healthy Team' who provide dry land alternatives to sailing and two administrators who look after accommodation, transfers, socials and many other things.

What qualities are you looking for when you employ instructors or beach staff?

Good sailing ability, hopefully with a background in racing, preferably on cats or skiffs. High wind ability is a must. They must also be friendly, approachable, self-starters and good team workers. Also, musical talent a plus!

How do you find new staff?

Mostly by word of mouth. I receive 50 or so job applications each year, but only a few will get accepted.

Are qualifications important?

Qualifications are important because we are an RYA Centre and want everyone to teach to RYA standards. Also, our insurance requires qualifications. For exceptional people, we may vary our requirements and give them RYA Assistant Instructor status – as a very old hand, I fall into that category myself!

What's the pay like? Do you pay more for staff who have qualifications and prior experience?

£80 a week for your first season including accommodation and some meals; other meals are subsidised. More experienced people can get paid substantially more.

How much time off does an instructor get? How many hours do they work?

One day off a week. Work hours are from 9.45 am to 7 pm each day with a break for lunch, plus helping with the weekly BBQ and some social occasions.

Good sailing ability, hopefully with a background in racing, preferably on cats or skiffs. High wind ability is a must.

Wildwind

The Watersweet Ocean Festival is all part of the Vassiliki lifestyle...

Could you describe a typical working day or working week at Wildwind?

Staff meeting 9.45, followed by preparation of boats, lectures and getting safety craft ready through to 10.30 when the centre opens. You then help clients rig their boats. We insist that clients do this – if something goes wrong, it may be vital to understand how the boat is rigged. We usually run a lecture in the morning and afternoon aimed at different levels, all the way from beginner stuff to kite handling in cats or skiffs in strong winds. On-the-water instruction is available, especially for beginners in the morning and for more experienced sailors during windy afternoons when we also run plenty of 'joy rides'. Then it's time for de-briefs and packing up boats. We also need a beach tower lookout during the whole day to co-ordinate safety boats. Weekly specials include a compulsory safety briefing for all clients on Mondays, race training day on Thursdays, regatta day on Fridays when staff help less experienced sailors take part in four races, sail-away excursion on Saturdays and maintenance on Sundays.

Do some people fail to make the grade?

I've only had to fire two in twenty years, both over incidents with girls!

What are the best things about working for a company like Wildwind? What are the worst things?

Best things are wonderful wind, great equipment, nice team, lots of sunshine, a committed approach, feedback from clients, improved skills, BBQ and the social life. The worst things are hangovers, long hours and occasional bad weather.

Anything else you would like to add?

There's nowhere else like Wildwind. No one lets you sail in Force 5-6's most days and has the performance kit to make the most of the conditions. Because of the wind and kit we attract the very best instructors. Our philosophy is that we are a sailing club away from home; we pride ourselves on our independence and a personal touch, both on and off the water.
■ www.wildwind.co.uk ❖

MINORCA SAILING HOLIDAYS – BALAERIC ISLANDS

Jeremy Evans

I an 'Basta' Aldridge is Beach Manager for Minorca Sailing Holidays. MSH has a superb line-up of dinghies, provides top class instruction at all levels from beginners to racers and high performance skiff sailors, and also provides a wide range of windsurfing gear with dedicated windsurf instructors.

Basta, how many dinghy and windsurfing instructors or helpers do you employ at Minorca Sailing during the high and low season?
During low season we have approximately 25 dinghy and windsurfing instructors. We employ more than twice as many for the summer peak season and autumn half term.

How much can a new employee expect to get paid?
We provide a competitive wage that increases with experience and the amount of time committed to working at our centre.

How many hours do your instructors work on average?
A typical working day is 8.30am - 6.30pm with an hour for lunch. All staff get one day off a week. Extra days off are given for 6 month staff, which increases each year you spend working at the sailing school.

What qualities are you looking for when you employ instructors or beach staff? Are qualifications important?
The RYA Dinghy and/or Windsurfing Instructor qualification is essential, accompanied with RYA L2 Powerboat and First Aid. We look to employ friendly, happy people who are willing to work hard and get enjoyment from their work. Previous experience at teaching is preferred.

How do you make sure your instructors are up to speed?
Training is provided, in the form of compulsory and voluntary clinics, to ensure all instructors have the opportunity to improve their skills.

Jeremy Evans

We look to employ friendly, happy people who are willing to work hard and get enjoyment from their work.

Rocketing along the Bay of Fornells with the sailing school in the background...

Jeremy Evans

Describe your own typical working day?

7:45. Get to work, check the weather and prepare the day's programme.

8:00. Liaise with senior instructors about the day's activities.

8:30. Group meeting with all the instructors for a full brief on the day.

8:30-10:00. Ensure the school set-up runs smoothly and is on time.

10:00. Day's briefing for all the guests.

10:30-13:00. Ensure the morning session is running safely and smoothly.

13:00-14:00. Lunch break for everyone.

14:00-16:30. Ensure the afternoon teaching sessions and races run safely and smoothly, while preparing the centre for personal tuition sessions.

16:30-18:30. Organise the personal tuition sessions which are one-to-one for an hour.

18:30. Prepare for the following day.

19:00. Go home and relax.

What are the best things about your job?

Best things are the location, the people I work with, watching clients enjoying themselves and coming off the water with a big smile, and seeing instructors progress throughout the season, both in their work and personal sailing or windsurfing experiences.

■ www.minorcasailing.co.uk ❖

Jeremy Evans

WINDSPORT – CORNWALL, UK

Jeremy Evans

Brian Phipps is the owner and principal of Windsport, a long established sailing school based in Falmouth Harbour. As a former champion cat sailor, Brian has carved a parallel career as an international catamaran trainer and coach, as well as branching out into product development, boat maintenance and new boat sales.

Brian, how would you describe your career?

On the water activity has been a large part of my life since I was a young lad, either canoeing, sailing, powerboating, surfing or making a raft! As a teenager, I was always keen to race whatever came my way and spent much of my spare time working as a sailing instructor. Teaching is a vocation that I both enjoy and came naturally from a early age. This combination of a passion for sailing with a determination that "Only the best will do" has led to a life of teaching and coaching, through to specialising in catamaran coaching via Windsport. Thirty-five years of working in sailing, teaching, training the trainers, international coaching and product development is a good start, but I still have loads to learn.

Can you explain why Windsport expanded into more than just a sailing school to make the business work?

Like any other business, Windsport has been changing with the times and the times have changed since we launched in1985. Windsport started as a specialist dinghy and catamaran sailing school with a policy and image that made us stand out from other sailing schools. The basic principles of attention to detail, combined with quality in boats, equipment and teaching has been at the heart of Windsport's success in other areas such as international coaching, product development, performance boat repairs and a facility for regatta and championship events. Our extensive dinghy park and rigging area means we can accommodate small or big fleets of dinghies or catamarans, with private customer boat parking and launching at all states of the tide.

What are the job opportunities with Windsport? How many instructors and other staff do you employ during the high and low season?

Windsport has expanded and contracted as the business has been steered through its various developments. At one time, we had three high profile schools in the UK with satellite centres abroad, but with the development of international coaching and development work, Windsport now only operates from our base at Mylor Harbour near Falmouth. We have a core team of staff that operate all year round, with a seasonal team who come back and work as part of the Windsport coaching team.

What qualities are you looking for when you employ people? How do you find them? Are qualifications or experience more important?

Legally we must have instructors with qualifications, but from a practical point of view experience does it all. We look to have a specialist in each area of the watersports we offer, with instructors having their own areas combined with other skills. Through staff training sessions we draw on each other's expertise. For instance, my expertise is coaching catamarans, so I will deliver a two hour staff session followed by a staff social BBQ debrief. This has two effects – sharing skills and bonding the team. Most staff training takes place after work so is an additional commitment, but our employees value the opportunity for skill development.

Could you describe a typical working day with your team at the Windsport sailing centre?

Staff briefing at 8.30 for instructors and everyone else, so we all know what each person will be doing, which needs to include any off-site coaching. Centre preparation and course detailing takes us through to 10.00am when the day's sailing courses get underway. At noon, the on-water staff touch base with each other and the chief instructor or any other management they need information from. The centre is shut down at the end of the day, leaving time to plan or adapt the next day's courses, do boat maintenance as required and have a group debrief.

Do some people fail to make the grade?

Most instructors are committed to being part of our professional team. If they are finding it difficult to match the quality we demand, it is our job to help them reach that standard, although it's a two-way process. If an instructor is not willing to plan and think ahead, look after equipment and show attention to detail, they will find working at Windsport does not fit with their understanding of being a professional instructor.

What are the advantages of working as an instructor in the UK, as opposed to somewhere that's sunny and glamorous like the Mediterranean?

Working in the UK is a challenge! We have a weather system that tests your instructing and coaching skills daily. No two days are the same, and that means flexibility and planning is paramount. The British are among the best all-round sailors in the world because they experience such a wide range of conditions. In my view the same applies to instructors who have taught professionally in the UK.

What are the best and worst things about working for a company like Windsport?

The best thing is being part of a professional team that has a lot of expertise and talent to draw on. You are always learning new skills and striving to deliver the best. The worst may depend on your view of being part of a professional team – if you are looking for an easy come, easy go kind of life, you may not appreciate the demands!

■ www.windsport.co.uk   ❖

Thirty-five years of working in sailing, teaching, training the trainers, international coaching and product development is a good start, but I still have loads to learn.

Jeremy Evans

Assistant Dinghy Instructor
Minimum Age: 14

■ **Requirements:** Recommended by RYA Principal; competent dinghy sailor; must have completed one of the RYA Sailing Scheme advanced modules.

■ **Useful qualifications:** RYA or MCA First Aid certificate; SRC radio certificate.
Becoming an Assistant Instructor is the first rung of the teaching ladder. You are qualified to assist dinghy instructors teaching up to Stage 3 standard courses, under the supervision of a Senior Instructor. Training and assessment are conducted by the principal or chief instructor of a training centre who will award AI certificates, which are valid at that centre for 5 years. Training is based on RYA teaching methods for beginners (RYA G14) and takes approximately 20 hours or 2 days.

Dinghy Instructor
Minimum Age: 16

■ **Requirements:** RYA or MCA First Aid certificate; RYA Powerboat Level 2 certificate; RYA Dinghy or Keelboat pre-entry assessment.

■ **Useful qualifications:** SRC radio certificate; RYA Safety Boat certificate; Advanced Dinghy certificates.
The RYA Dinghy Instructor qualification is fundamental to being paid to work at a sailing school. Pre-entry assessment of sailing ability is required to take the course. The assessment normally lasts half a day, but may be part of a two day refresher course. Primary skills are sailing manoeuvres and theory, which may include sailing backwards and rudderless sailing. The RYA Dinghy Instructor course lasts a full five days and is extremely intensive with continuous assessment, teaching candidates how to run on-water sessions and deliver shore-based talks. An RYA Dinghy Instructor is qualified to teach Levels 1 and 2, Day Sailing and Seamanship Skills, plus Sailing with Spinnakers if approved by the principal or chief instructor.

Jeremy Evans

Advanced Dinghy Instructor

Minimum Age: 16

■ **Requirements:** RYA or MCA First Aid certificate; RYA Powerboat Level 2 certificate; RYA Dinghy Instructor.

■ **Useful qualifications:** SRC radio certificate; RYA Safety Boat certificate.

An Advanced Dinghy Instructor is an experienced instructor who has been trained to teach Performance Sailing and Sailing with Spinnakers courses. The two day Advanced Dinghy Instructor course is based on continuous assessment, which includes powerboat handling while teaching, and may include a theory test.

Racing Instructor

Minimum Age: 16

■ **Requirements:** RYA or MCA First Aid certificate; RYA Powerboat Level 2 certificate; RYA Dinghy Instructor.

■ **Useful qualifications:** SRC radio certificate; RYA Safety Boat certificate.

Instructors with experience of club racing can teach racing skills through the Start Racing module of the RYA Sailing Scheme. The one day course will include organisation of club racing, preparation and management of the Start Racing course and instructional techniques afloat including race training exercises.

Multihull or Keelboat Instructor

Minimum Age: 16

■ **Requirements:** RYA or MCA First Aid certificate; RYA Powerboat Level 2 certificate; RYA Dinghy Instructor.

■ **Useful qualifications:** SRC radio certificate; RYA Safety Boat certificate.

An intensive two day course with continuous assessment is required for the endorsement to teach multihull or keelboat sailing.

Senior Instructor

Minimum Age: 18

■ **Requirements:** Recommended by RYA Principal; RYA or MCA First Aid certificate; RYA Powerboat Level 2 certificate; RYA Safety Boat certificate; RYA Dinghy Instructor; two seasons or one year full time instructing.

■ **Useful qualifications:** SRC radio certificate.

An intensive four day course for experienced instructors who wish to organise and manage courses, taking responsibilty for the work of instructors and assistant instructors. An RYA recognised training centre must have a Senior Instructor (SI) as its principal or chief instructor.

SUMMER HOLIDAY INSTRUCTOR – HOME AND ABROAD

Working as a sailing instructor in the south of England and south of France showed Miles Handley that different things make it good to work at home and abroad…

Hi Miles, how many jobs have you had as a sailing instructor?

I've had two summer holiday jobs. I worked for Rockley Watersports in Poole on the South Coast UK for the summer holidays in 2007 and for PGL in Mimosa, South of France for summer 2008.

What experience and qualifications did you need to get those jobs?

I qualified as an RYA Dinghy Instructor. Before starting this qualification I had experience of dinghy sailing and racing and several RYA dinghy sailing certificates. Then the senior instructor at my sailing club, Chipstead SC, asked if I was interested in joining a RYA Dinghy Sailing Instructor course they were running. I thought this would be a good way of getting qualified for part-time work at sailing schools. The course involved theory, first aid and powerboat operation. I did most of the course at Chipstead on weekends and completed it with a one-week course at a commercial sailing school.

What are the good and bad points about working as an instructor?

I like working outside on the water and beach when the weather is good. Most people enjoy themselves on courses, so working with them is fun and you can become good friends with other instructors. It is also rewarding teaching people to sail – good to be able to pass on experience and watch them develop their skills. However, the hours can be very long and the rate of pay is not very high compared to some other summer jobs. When the weather is bad working outside is sometimes not so much fun, but the good days make up for this.

How did a summer season at Rockley compare with a summer season at PGL? How would you rate the main attractions of working in the UK and working abroad?

There were advantages and disadvantages at both venues. In the UK the rates of pay are generally higher, accommodation is a little better and there are no language barriers, plus you get a few days' holiday to go home or catch up with friends. In the South of France most days were hot and sunny and I was working on perfect sandy beaches, which was quite a contrast to the UK. It was also interesting to work abroad for the first time. I gained experience working with people of different nationalities, although instructors were all from the UK.

Jeremy Evans

A summer job as a sailing instructor in the sun combines the healthy outdoors with an interesting lifestyle. You can live with the minimal pay providing joy rides like this...

What is the pay like? Can you cover your expenses, and even build up some savings, by working as an instructor?

The hourly rate of pay for a sailing instructor is not very high when you are on basic rates, but the rates go up with experience and repeated seasons with the same company and with age – over 21 in the UK. My expenses were very low as I was living in provided accommodation with food costs also covered, so all my income was saved.

Vital Reading: G14 RYA Dinghy Coaching Handbook and Logbook.

Would you recommend a summer season as an instructor? What advice – in terms of getting the right qualifications and choosing the best job – would you give to someone who wants to give it a go?

Yes, I would recommend a summer job as a sailing instructor – it's in the healthy outdoors and more interesting than most summer work. You need the necessary experience to undertake and pass the sailing instructor course, which also requires money and time. But even if you don't have the experience to get this certificate, it can still be possible to work as an assistant sailing instructor or general helper at a sailing school. ❖

All part of a day's work.
Dan Jaspers launches the RS Vision.

Jeremy Evans

DINGHY SAILING
WORKING IN THE BUSINESS

One way of getting paid to sail, or at least talk and think about sailing, is to work in production, marketing, design or management. Opportunities are widespread in the dinghy world.

EXPAND YOUR PASSION – Dan Jaspers

Dan Jaspers worked as a sailing instructor, school teacher, lecturer, yacht worker and first mate with the America's Cup Solent Experience, before taking charge of corporate sales and training fleet development with RS Sailing.

Hi Dan, can you describe how you work?

With over 1,400 clients throughout the UK and abroad and with nearly a quarter of the market share, I cater for a very diverse range of schools, centres and holiday clubs. The job was created when I had extensive talks with RS about broadening their introductory APB (All Purpose Boats) range, which doubled over the next two years, and approaching institutions. I am involved with every stage of new boat design, development and final use of the RS schools range.

My job involves a great deal of travel, sometimes getting up at 02:00 to drive to the North of England to demonstrate a boat to a club, then turn round and drive all the way back on the same day. On other occasions I may spend five days visiting clubs in one region, doing a series of open days with up to four boats on my trailer or the roof of my van. The team at work will never forget the week when I clocked over 1,500 miles and drove to every possible corner of the UK. Good times!

The other crucial part of my job is attending all the RYA conferences, which are split into regions and attract up to 100 dinghy instructors, club managers and training centre principals and are a great time to make contact. Regional Development Officers host these one-day conferences to update the regions on news from the trade and from the RYA. Competition is fierce between RS and the other two main manufacturers, but I thrive off this. We also use the feedback I get from all the attendees to develop our boats further, which is valuable in keeping the company at the forefront of design evolution.

I am also an RYA Coach/Assessor, working freelance to provide Instructor, Senior Instructor and Advanced Instructor training across the country. An exciting project has been a worldwide scheme for Personal Instructor Development, using online e-learning resources and more traditional practical sailing courses to bridge the link between instructors and potential coaches. The focus is on 'soft' skills helping instructors to build up a coaching dialogue with their students, requiring a very different set of skills from instructional qualities taught at basic level. As we rely on sailors becoming 'self aware' we need to unlock the links between personal experience and personal development.

The fact that every one of my clients is different and needs to be treated uniquely, means my style of delivery has to be flexible.

How would you rate your job?

It's a great job, but what makes it special is that it is organic. I have so much leeway surrounding the 'sales' part of my role that it is not uncommon to spend a day with the development team, looking at new reefing systems for a particular boat, or talking to maritime students at college or university about the watersports industry. The fact that every one of my extensive list of clients is different and needs to be treated uniquely, means my style of delivery has to be flexible. A 'hard sell' will not work on seasoned veterans of the outdoor education world, who need to be persuaded by how good the kit is and what it can offer to youngsters and adults. With commercial managers I switch into a very different mode. Residual values of boats and bi-annual replacement schemes for fleet rotation will normally be discussed, as everything is much more revenue and price oriented.

The bad points of the job are kissing goodbye to weekends, since many clubs are not open during the week. It is quite usual for me to work three out of four and sometimes every weekend during the peak months of February to April. Driving mileage is also a love/hate relationship. I regularly do 1,000 miles a week, mainly during the hours of darkness. The trick is to have a good selection on the iPod, a good Sat Nav and a comfy vehicle. I was fortunate enough to get a lovely van as part of my job package – it's the thing I treasure most of all the perks.

Paper chasing is all too common, but in reality those bits of paper do not prepare an instructor for the 'What if?' scenario.

LDC Racing Sailboats

Jeremy Evans

I was head hunted by the America's Cup Solent Experience team, who offered me the job of Bowman on France 2 and France 3. Climbing those 120 foot masts for daily rig checks was the highlight of my first season!

How did you start your sailing career?

I don't come from a sailing family. My mother discovered yacht sailing when I was 12 and I grew interested in this whole new lifestyle. There was a note on the school notice board asking students to sign up for a youth group visit to an Outdoor Education Centre in Chichester Harbour, so I saved my paper round money to pay for an amazing weekend. The instructors were so good that I got the whole idea of ropes and sails and invisible force very quickly. I couldn't wait to go again and by 1997 had all my dinghy certificates and was ready to do my instructor course. This led to working at Cobnor Activities Centre during the summer holidays, making some lifelong friends in the process. My commitment to sailing was apparent, as my

university lecturer asked if I was going to be a 'professional beach bum' or use my talents studying graphic design for a future career. The answer was simple… I would do both.

I graduated and worked the following year as chief instructor at the centre, having completed my Senior Dinghy Instructor and Powerboat Instructor courses. During this time I also applied for PGCE Teacher Training in Outdoor Education and Art/Design at the University of Bangor, and with a glowing reference from the local Outdoor Education Advisor for Sussex had an unconditional offer for the next academic year. My plan to combine a love of the outdoors, especially sailing, with a career was coming together.

How did your career develop?

After the PGCE, I worked as an art teacher at an all boys school, with responsibility for setting up an Outdoor Education programme. Worries about litigation and issues regarding off-site visits prevented me from doing what I knew the pupils would love, so I left to teach the BTEC National Diploma in Sport Studies at Chichester College, with special emphasis on developing sailing.

That was wonderful, but the call of the water was too great and I took a job with Sunsail at their Port Solent base. I had been interested in yachts for a while and simply wanted to see how they compared to dinghies. The move was easier than I expected. As a dinghy sailor, you learn about wind shifts and are constantly adjusting sails. Yacht sailors generally do not bother, so with this extra knowledge I was soon doing very well in the weekly staff races. So much so that I was head hunted by the America's Cup Solent Experience team, who offered me the job of Bowman on their two ex-San Diego 1995 IACC boats, France 2 and France 3. Climbing those 120 foot masts for daily rig checks was the highlight of my first season! The second season saw me move further back to become a First Mate in charge of crew and clients, translating the skipper's wishes into reality. With a team of 22 to organise, I was in my element. Nothing in comparison to the 30 rowdy teenagers I had to contend with a couple of years before, except that these million pound yachts were not very forgiving if things went wrong. Having qualified as a Commercially Endorsed Yachtmaster, I was also able to take the wheel on occasion and put my dinghy skills into play. The Cup Boats performed exactly the same as a 15 foot performance dinghy… absolutely incredible! Sailing upwind at 18 degrees to the apparent wind and flying 520 square metre masthead kites during the Round the Island race and Cowes Week will be etched in my memory for ever. At the end of my second season, the America's Cup boats were sold and I had to find work over the winter, which is low point time for any seasonal sailor. Painting pub windows, laying turf in pouring rain and fitting bathrooms during the freezing months of winter will never rate as my idea of fun. Luckily, my best friend was working for RS and found me a job building Fevas. That was the beginning of where we are now. I saw a way to make things on the boats more effective and when It came to the end of my temporary contract, I suggested that RS needed someone to look after training. Having become an RYA Coach/Assessor, whilst working on the America's Cup boats, I was well placed to be the industry eye for a young, progressive company in a fast moving market.

Without friends and contacts, you are another CV in a big pile, so being aware of this from the outset and not making enemies is crucial.

How do you rate qualifications, experience and being in the right place at the right time?

Nobody is anything without experience. Far too many believe that just because they have one certificate, they can automatically get all the others. Paper chasing is all too common, but in reality those bits of paper do not prepare an instructor for the 'What if?' scenario. The ability to be able to see a situation unfolding and react 'pro-actively' as opposed to 'reactively' can only come from having spent time on the water teaching or sailing. Mother nature has so many variables and the nature of humans is that we are predictable in our unpredictability, so it makes sense that a group of kids will inevitably do something potentially dangerous in any session. Good outdoor instructors can sense this and lessen the impact.

Qualifications are helpful for getting jobs, but the personality and ability to do the task comes into play much more than any office job, with all candidates undertaking probationary periods or running mock sessions to have their ability judged. Those who apply for work with every ticket under the sun, acquired within a few months at the same training establishment, will no doubt get more of a 'too good to be true' response from the employer. The relevance of qualifications on a CV is also something to watch out for. If you are going for a straightforward instructor position, is it wise to send a CV with every other ticket listed including the mountaineering badge from a Scout trip to the Alps, or reserve it for interview when asked about your other skills and attributes?

Once you have the experience, contacts and 'industry friends' become more useful than I can ever emphasise. It is such a small community that people you work with may progress to manage a club, run a holiday company, take marine photos, edit yachting publications, teach outdoor education at a College or University or work for the RYA. Without friends and contacts, you are another CV in a big pile, so being aware of this from the outset and not making enemies is crucial.

What advice would you give to someone who wants to work on the water?

Unless you are working in a managerial position, or for a non-commercial operation such as an outdoor centre that keeps active all year, most instructing jobs are on offer from March through to October, with many young people chasing winter ski seasons or applying for sailing jobs in the Caribbean. My advice is to have more strings to your bow. Find other activities which can be taught during the winter months or have regular temping to fall back on.

Watersport jobs in general do not pay large salaries, even though the work can be hard. Your bonus will come from perks such as cheaper holidays, food and accommodation provided by the employer, cost price sailing kit, free access to boats at clubs and schools, on-the-job qualifications free in exchange for commitment to work, free crewing opportunities on yachts which others have to pay for, being outdoors all day long, a year round tan, a healthy life, meeting different people every day and learning skills that others would love to learn.

Remember to keep yourself up to date. If you stagnate, others with more passion and ideas will not be far behind. The one thing that has to remain is your passion for the sport. It's easy to forget how amazing everything is when you do it every day.

■ www.rssailing.com ❖

After three busy years running the Training and Fleet Sales department at RS, Dan Jaspers was offered the new post of Training and Development Manager at the International Sailing Federation, with a brief to develop ISAF's worldwide Connect to Sailing programme, working with national authorities and building grass roots training to feed into Olympic success.

THE BOAT BUILDER – LodayWhite Catamarans

White Formula

Henry White comes from a sailing and boatbuilding dynasty, founded by his grandfather Reg White who won an Olympic gold medal in the catamaran class at the 1976 Olympics. Having completed a three year boatbuilding course at Lowestoft College, Henry gradually took over the running of LodayWhite Catamarans.

Henry, can you give us the background to your career and explain what your work involves?

It all started when I made my first daggerboard around the age of eight. I always knew I wanted to be a boatbuilder, so I worked at the factory with my dad every day after school, but like everyone I had to start at the bottom, making cups of tea and sweeping the floors as I slowly worked my way up. After three years doing a boatbuilding course at Lowestoft College, I starting working with Reg White at LodayWhite Catamarans, then took over when he retired. Now, I'm building boats and sailing all over the world.

Is that a great job? What are the good points? There must be some bad points as well…

It's an amazing job! The best thing is that I sail high performance catamarans at all the big events and get paid for it. Bad points? I can't honestly think of any!

Do you sail a lot? Does the fact that it's work ever spoil sailing for you?

Yeah loads, more than ever. The fact that it's work just makes me realise how lucky I am.

How has your career developed over the years? What have been the highlights?

I've seen myself move up from making tea and coffee to making boats, which is pretty cool when you look back and see how far you've come in a few years. The highlight has to be working with my dad Rob on our new Formula 18, and listening to my grand-dad's Olympic Tornado stories!

Jeremy Evans

What qualifications do you have? Would you recommend a boatbuilding course as a good way to start a career in sailing?

I have all my City and Guilds qualifications in boat building and all my NVQs – in fact I've got more certificates than a doctor! The course in Lowestoft was free to join and taught traditional boatbuilding. That's good, as you still need those skills for modern day boatbuilding, though I may have broken the mould when I started making my 14 foot carbon skiff! A boatbuilding course is certainly a good way to get into a

sailing career, as there are many jobs available in this field all around the world.

How important has sailing and regatta experience been for your career?

They are so important, because I need to be at all the events to show off the boats, plus it helps me to get faster and faster each time I race. You can also understand a boat a lot more, when you can see things both from the building and sailing side.

Would you recommend becoming a boatbuilder? How would you rate working with wooden boats, high performance racing machines or mass volume rotomoulding?

Definitely, it's such a cool job. It's great working in all the different fields of boatbuilding, but I enjoy high performance stuff the most!

What advice would you give to someone who wants to follow your type of career?

All you need do is get yourself into a boatbuilding college, or find a suitable job and do lots of sailing. This helps you to understand all the basics of what makes a boat work. So start playing around with a boat for fun and see where you go for there.

How would you like your own career to develop?

I would like to continue sailing as a career and get better and bigger in the sailing world, but as long as I'm sailing I'll be happy.

Anything you would like to add?

In life you either Go Big or Go Home!

■ **www.lodaywhite.com** ❖

LOWESTOFT COLLEGE

Boat Construction, Maintenance and Support.

City and Guilds Level 2 – 1 year full time.

■ This course is designed to provide the background knowledge and practical experience required within boatbuilding and the marine leisure industry. Students work towards the City and Guilds 2451 Boat Construction Maintenance and Support and EMTA EAL performing engineering operations qualifications. Successful completion provides a broad knowledge of the required skills to progress to industry or to the next level of this course. Applicants should demonstrate an aptitude for wood and boat craft skills and the interest and ability to cope with the demands of the course.

Boat Construction, Maintenance and Support.

City and Guilds Level 3 – 1 year full time.

■ This course is aimed at students who are employed or intend to gain employment in a boatyard or within the marine leisure industry. The course includes health and safety, engineering drawing and lofting skills. **Units:** Safe and effective working in a boatbuilding, repair and service environment. Boatbuilding repair and service materials in technology. **Optional units:** Production and finishing of hulls and decks. Producing and fitting structural components.

■ **More information:** Lowestoft College, St Peters Street, Lowestoft, Suffolk NR32 2NB.
Tel: 01502 500031 · email: info@lowestoft.ac.uk · web: www.lowestoft.ac.uk

Andrew Barratt

SELLING A DREAM – Jon Manners

Jeremy Evans

Jon Manners is Senior Sales Manager, with direct responsibility for new boat sales, across the Topper International range of dinghies and cats.

Jon, can you describe your job with Topper Sailboats?
My job involves setting sales targets with the Sales Director, developing leads for corporate clients in the UK and overseas, as well as dealing with private buyers in the UK which requires attending boat shows and taking clients for test sails. Providing feedback for our Technical Director is also important, ranging from existing products to sailing school adaptations and new boats being developed.

How does your work change throughout the year, from January through to December?
The year always starts with a series of boat shows in the UK and overseas, finishing with Sailboat at Alexandra Palace in March. During this time we are working with schools to develop their fleets, commissioning new boats and working with the RYA on regional instructor conferences. As we move past Easter, the majority of school orders are delivered and the focus of the UK market shifts to private buyers, requiring many test sails and commissioning

all the new boats bought by clients. Things get quieter by the start of August, leaving more time to provide support at big events like the annual Topper World Championship. Then we move back into show season which starts at Southampton during September, while still keeping busy with dispatching boats worldwide. The final quarter is spent working with schools on plans for the following year, as well as taking boats to them for testing. We will also be involved with testing and development of new products and final deliveries of clients' boats.

Can you describe a typical working week during the summer?
An average week will be split between time at our main office at Ashford, our demo centre at Datchet Water and on the road visiting sailing events or clients. Emails need to be checked and followed up every day, as well as speaking with my team and sales director. A day in the office will involve time on the phone and computer, as well as forward planning meetings; a day at the demo centre or on the road will involve demo sails with clients and commissioning new boats.

What qualities do you need for your work? Are qualifications or experience most important?
I am an RYA Senior Instructor, which certainly helps, but the main requirement for the job is to be good with people and able to listen to what they are saying. It also requires good attention to detail, being well organised and a willingness to do whatever job is needed at the time.

Do you employ seasonal staff to help out?
We occasionally employ qualified dinghy instructors to work at boat shows and events or take people sailing.

Jeremy Evans

The best things are getting out on the water and sailing at any time of the year, introducing new people to a sport I love and having a job that is never the same from one day to the next

What opportunities do you get to go sailing? Are there perks connected with the job?

The sailing is not as great as people might expect. Most of the time I'm doing demo sails which requires a controlled, safe style of sailing. The main perk is that I can enjoy occasional freesailing with any boat in the range I fancy. It's also great to have the opportunity to meet so many enthusiastic and famous people connected with sailing.

What are the best and worst things about your job?

The best things are getting out on the water and sailing at any time of the year, introducing new people to a sport I love and having a job that is never the same from one day to the next. The worst part could be all the driving, but I don't

mind as it gives me time to think and plan. That leaves rigging and derigging boats, which has to be the worst part of my job in freezing rain or snow!

How did you get your job?

I got into the marine trade by accident, through doing a windsurfing instructor course and working part time at sailing centres on my days off. This led to working for Topper at a boat show where I sold some boats and had a good time. They asked me back to do more shows, then asked me to run their new demo centre full time, which led to becoming sales manager.

Would you recommend the marine trade?

You may not get mega rich and the hours can be long and involve full weekends, but you will have a good time! ❖

THE DIRECTOR'S VIEW – Martin Wadhams

LDC Racing Sailboats

Martin Wadhams is managing director of RS Sailing and LDC Racing Sailboats.

What qualities are you looking for when you employ people?
Experience in sailing or on the job are important, often more than qualifications. Having said that, there are some qualifications which are very relevant to our business.

Do you employ seasonal staff?
Most of our staff are permanent, but we add one or two to our workshop and parts sales teams during their busiest times.

What opportunities do staff get to go sailing? Are there perks connected with the job?
Opportunities to go sailing as part of work apply to sales staff, who are involved with demonstrations, and to boat development staff during new model and equipment testing. We also have demonstration boats for most of our range and encourage staff to sail and race them at club and RS events.

What is your busiest time of year? Could you describe a typical working day or working week at RS when it's flat out?
The busiest times vary from one area of the business to another. The sales team are probably busiest during the boat shows. These are intensive times and involve building stands at UK shows, as well as manning them when they're open. Our workshop team is busiest in the spring – March to May being the peak. We do not build the boats in-house, but final preparation to customer's order, PDI (pre-delivery inspection) and loading for delivery to international dealers are all time consuming and very important jobs. The parts sales team are busy in the spring and then get stretched during the summer championship season, especially as we aim to provide a parts back-up service at major RS events.

Jeremy Evans

The Q'ba was developed as part of the RS all purpose range.

The best thing for the right enthusiast is working with motivated and enthusiastic colleagues in a sport that most of us love. The worst times are when something goes wrong.

Jeremy Evans

Martin takes a ride in the RS500, part of the RS high performance range.

Do some people fail to make the grade when they work for you? What goes wrong?

We have many long term staff, but of course a few fail to make the grade. One 'high risk' area we have noticed is when people have finished education and start their first job. There can be a shock element before the realisation sets in that the world does not owe them a living – they need to settle into the routine of working hard for five days a week! A few leave us before they work this out, and then find out the hard way that the grass is not necessarily greener elsewhere! We do try to enjoy our work along the way. Having like minded colleagues and customers makes it a great environment for those who come to appreciate the contrast with many other jobs out there!

■ **www.ldcracingsailboats.co.uk**

What are the best things about working for a company like RS ? What are the worst things?

The best thing for the right enthusiast is working with motivated and enthusiastic colleagues in a sport that most of us love. Our customers are also enthusiastic as we are dealing with something they want to do. The worst times are when something goes wrong. We all hate making mistakes, or being let down, when the knock-on effect adversely affects our customers. They are not anonymous people. We know many of them well, deal with them for many years, sail and socialise together, so there is a much closer relationship than many businesses have with their customers. This is great when things go well, but can be hard if things go wrong. It brings increased responsibility and greater satisfaction from doing a good job. ❖

DESIGNER & CONSULTANT – Paul Handley

Jeremy Evans

Paul Handley designed the RS K6 racing keelboat, followed by the extremely popular RS Feva, Tera and Q'BA which are produced in rotomoulded plastic. His other designs include the Mustang 30 yacht.

Paul, can you give us the background to your career and work?

I'm a naval architect and I specialise mainly in small pleasure boats. Boat design is part of my work, but I have always worked as a consultant naval architect as well. I work independently from home and in recent years have concentrated on designing several dinghies that have become new classes, including the RS Feva and Tera.

Is that a great job?

It's a good job most of the time, but like all jobs some tasks are more mundane than others. Certainly it's exciting to design and develop a new boat and watch it grow into a successful new class, but that doesn't happen very often. As a consultant some jobs are interesting

– believe it or not, meetings which develop international stability or construction standards can sometimes get exciting!

How did you get started?

I used to race Half-Tonner yachts in the Solent with my family when I was a teenager and grew interested in the IOR (International Offshore Rule) and yacht design. When it came to choosing a career, I looked into naval architecture and found I could qualify with a degree in Ship Science at Southampton University. As Southampton was near to the Solent, this seemed like a good idea!

How has your career developed over the years? What have been the important breaks?

I began at the Wolfson Unit at Southampton University. This was a great start, as within weeks of joining I was working alongside leading yacht designers tank testing America's Cup yachts. I also got involved in the post 1979 Fastnet Race disaster research on yacht capsizes, which was to prove useful later in my career when working on safety standards. Then I left to work as technical reporter for a yachting magazine. This was a bit of a career change, but helping to test boats I had previously tank-tested with the Wolfson Unit was good experience.

After that, I had a go at working from home and designed the Mustang 30 as a production club racer. It became a successful Channel Handicap (IRC) racer and I might have gone on to design more yachts, but instead took a full-time position with the International Yacht Racing Union (now known as ISAF). This provided an interesting insight into the world of international yachting politics and a good opportunity to meet and work with top boat builders. The highlight was providing technical support at the 1992 Olympic Regatta.

Paul's K6 design at full speed. After a slow start, this small keelboat became a great success.

My next move was to become a Consultant for the European Commission, assisting with the development of ISO safety standards that support the EU Recreational Craft Directive (RCD). Most of my time was spent on the development of ISO standards for yacht stability, design and construction. Getting this position was perhaps my best career break, as it was part-time working from home, with one or two days a week free for other consultancy or boat design.

I decided to take this opportunity to push to get some new designs into production and took a small keelboat design to Rondar, which eventually became the RS K6. Shortly after I approached RS with the Feva design and have worked a lot with them since.

Thinking about your career, how important are qualifications, experience, ability, contacts and being in the right place at the right time?

I think that qualifications, experience, ability,

contacts and timing have all been important at different times in my career. A degree in naval architecture was all important for my first job, but I moved to Motorboat and Yachting magazine because they liked an article I had written on yacht capsizing and were looking for a technical reporter.

There's no doubt that contacts help when it comes to getting new boat designs into production, but you are unlikely to get a company to back a new product unless they are really convinced by the design. So you must have the necessary depth of experience to produce a sound design and be prepared to go back to the drawing board if it isn't right first time. For instance, I designed and built three prototypes over several years for a junior single-handed dinghy, which eventually became the RS Tera, and did a lot of work getting it into production. Since then I've helped build class activity – it was very rewarding to see 50 boats at the World Championship in Sweden just two years after the launch.

What advice would you give to someone who wants to make a living from sailing by working as a yacht or dinghy designer?

I'm not sure that I should describe yacht and dinghy design as a 'sensible career', but if you are very determined and have both a passion and eye for design, then you should be able to earn a living as a designer and some people will get the big breaks and do very well. Also a knowledge of yacht design can be very useful for a number of related jobs, such as boat building, consultancy, boat surveying, sailmaking, marine journalism, marine materials and structural expertise, as well as general marine equipment design and manufacture. So there are plenty of opportunities to move into a career that enables a sailing enthusiast to combine work and pleasure.

The Tera, Q'ba and Feva are part of the RS all purpose range designed by Paul Handley.

However, it is likely to be hard to earn a living solely from designing small boats and dinghies. Every dinghy designer I know has also worked in a connected activity such as boatbuilding, consultancy or design of bigger yachts. In recent years, there has also been a large expansion in the construction of superyachts, generating a lot of jobs and providing a very good income for some designers, but this trend may not continue.

What is the best way to get started? What courses or colleges/universities would you recommend?

To be a yacht designer you don't have to qualify as a naval architect, nor is a degree in yacht design required, but it may be hard to get your first job without such a qualification. If you plan to take on a naval architecture degree, you should have a sound academic background in maths and science. To qualify as a Member of the Royal Institution of Naval Architects and as a Chartered Engineer, you normally need an accredited degree and up to six years' experience in a relevant job. This professional qualification is not required for yacht design, but is likely to help for consultant naval architects.

Southampton University offers a naval architecture degree called Ship Science and a fourth year option on Yacht and Small Craft Design. Naval architecture degrees focusing mainly on ship design and offshore engineering can also be taken at University College London, Newcastle University and Strathclyde/Glasgow University. Southampton Solent University focuses on yacht design and production with degrees for Yacht and Powercraft Design and for Yacht Production and Surveying. Plymouth University offers a marine materials degree called Marine and Composites Technology and even a degree in Surf Science and Technology!

How would you like your career to develop?

When I started out I decided to specialise in small craft for as long as I could earn a reasonable living, preferably with some design activity. I'm happy with a mix of consultancy and design and hope to design a few more small boats and dinghies, perhaps also some larger boats. I like the idea of writing about boats again and possibly getting more involved in production and boat building, but would need the right product at the right time. ❖

LIFE AS A SAILMAKER – Andy Davis

Speed Sails

Andy is head of the sail loft at Speed Sails. He specialises in making championship-winning sails for a wide range of dinghies including International Moths, where he won the National and European junior titles, and Solo where he won the UK, Welsh and Dutch National titles. He also races at the top of the fleet in Scorpions, GP14s and Merlin Rockets, while developing new sail designs.

How I learned to make sails…
I started at Speed Sails in 2001, straight after school as a trainee sailmaker. At first my main duties were to patch sails, stick on numbers, put in eyelets and check over sails before they were dispatched. Gradually, I was shown the complete sailmaking process from start to finish. It was when I started racing the Solo and Scorpion that I got more involved in sail design and began to understand the mechanics of a

sail. I then applied this knowledge to the general sailmaking process I had learnt, adding my own craftsmanship. Being responsible for sails at Speed encouraged me to develop innovative designs throughout all classes. It has also enabled me to be more involved in the business side of running a sail loft.

The skills you need…
Sailmaking is an art. You need an innate feel for the shape of a sail. You must instinctively be able to tell whether a sail will be too full or too flat when it is rigged. Understanding the sailmaking process and knowing how shape is put into a sail, and then going out sailing, gives you a good eye for great sails. The science behind a successful sail is obviously important, but the skills, expertise and experience of the sailmaker are the key.

Sailmakers also need to be able to cut straight! The other necessary skill is being able to competently use a sewing machine! Working with different types of cloth is important and being able to adapt designs for particular clients is the key to ultimate commercial success.

Learning by your mistakes…
Throughout history, sailmaking has developed through trial and improvement. It takes a long time to learn the art and experience makes mistakes less likely, but you always have to be pushing boundaries to make a sail that is a little bit better. Without errors there would be no progress. Or as Yoda in Star Wars explained, "If there is do and do not there is no try!"

The science behind a successful sail is obviously important, but the skills, expertise and experience of the sailmaker are the key.

Speed Sails

Winning races…

It certainly helps to sell your product if you win a lot of races, but it's not necessary to be a top racer in order to make good sails. For that, you need a good understanding of the dynamics of a sail, the cloth, the cut and the design. However, if people see you out there consistently at the front of the fleet, it gives them confidence in the sails you make. Events can be used to showcase your sails and talk to potential clients about their requirements.

Testing, testing, testing…

Testing sails is very important, just like any other product. From a business point of view, our testing has to take place at weekends during one-on-one tuning sessions.

Marketing matters…

Being out on the circuit talking to your customers is the best way to advertise your sails. The sails can be seen in action and clients can discuss individual needs with you face to face. We also use other good sailors to promote our sails across a range of different classes. The more sails we have at the front of the fleet, the more people will want to buy them! Having world or national titles to back up your designs is an obvious advantage.

■ **www.speedsails.co.uk**

Customers need educating…

It's important to close the gap in knowledge between a professional sailmaker and customers who sail as a recreational pursuit. We provide a tuning guide with every Speed sail, helping the customer set up the rig for optimum performance. Generally people are aware of their own sailing ability and I try to match a sail to a client's needs. The door is always open for people to come and ask for help and advice. I always try to talk to customers about their individual sails when I meet them at events.

Hard graft…

Sailmaking is fairly physically demanding, but not just for the young! Anyone of average fitness could cope with the workload. You are required to switch between standing up and kneeling down a lot, which can create knee problems. I don't suffer yet, but may need to get some special kneepads in a few years' time! I only get to sit down when I'm designing or digitising at the computer, which probably equates to about 10% of my time at work. All that standing is a bit tough on the legs and feet when you first start, but you get used to it.

Best things about sailmaking
■ The satisfaction of seeing your designs and hard work out on the water winning events!
■ Working with and helping your customers.
■ Working in your favourite sporting industry.

Worst things about sailmaking
■ Long hours before the championship season – when sails are in high demand, working life becomes a seven-day week.

Perks of the job
■ My sailing expenses are paid for.
■ I can use and test new equipment.
■ I get time off normal work to compete in national championships.   ❖

The fruit of expertise, passion and hard graft – a new suit of Speed Sails made by Andy Davis for the Merlin Rocket dinghy.

Jeremy Evans

WINNING RACES & SELLING SAILS

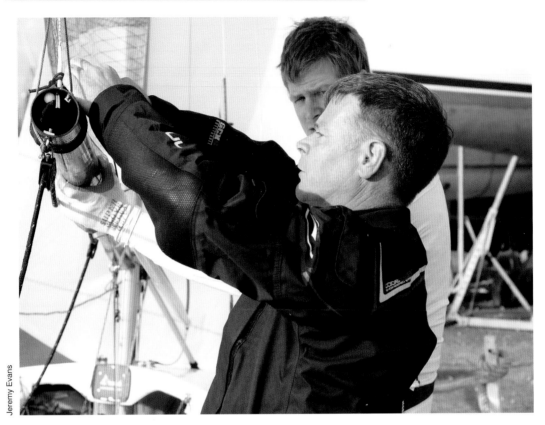

Jeremy Evans

Pinnell & Bax has grown from a sailmaker to a full-service global sailing business. Co-partner Ian Pinnell has won more than 50 world, European and national sailing championships.

Ian, what skills does a sailmaker require?

I guess you need to be practical, with a good eye for sails and a lot of experience. Being a good sailor helps enormously so you can focus on boat speed, with a good understanding of how masts bend and their moments of inertia. Sailmaking is not an exact science, but has general principles. I suspect that designing sails for yachts is easier than designing for dinghies, since the requirements can be quite different from one class to another.

How do you market P&B sails?

By racing, going fast through having the best designs and talking in the bar!

How do you ensure customers understand how to get the best out of their sails?

We supply tuning guides wherever possible. Rig set-up is crucial, but a lot of people either haven't got the eye or the knowledge. The service we offer includes making sure this is correct. If customers want to know why they are not going faster, we sort out where they have gone wrong with the rig.

Your knees must take a pounding from making sails?

We try and work on benches as much as possible, so we have a specially made jib bench, mainsail bench and benches for other sails. Some larger sails have to be made on the floor, so kneepads are the order for the day!

What are the best and worst things about working as sailmaker?

Good life style. You get to meet lots of people and talk about your hobby all the time. Quite often it turns out to be a 7 days a week job, but if sailing is your passion you generally get to use the best kit and it shouldn't cost you anything.

Would you recommend sailmaking as a career?

Yes, but don't expect to get rich. It's hard work, like any business should be, but very enjoyable.

Jeremy Evans

Quite often it turns out to be a 7 days a week job, but if sailing is your passion you generally get to use the best kit and it shouldn't cost you anything.

■ **www.pinbax.com**

Powering upwind in a P&B 505, shortly after winning the world championships.

Jeremy Evans

SAILING

WORKING AS A PROFESSIONAL RACER

4

Being paid to work as a professional racer sounds too good to be true. The advantage is that you can make a good living, while doing what you love best. The disadvantage is that this kind of career is only open to the most talented and determined sailors, as our case histories show.

RYA Skandia GBR

Paul Campbell-James and Mark Asquith out in the 'office'.

OLYMPIC SAILOR – Andrea Brewster

RYA Skandia GBR

Andrea started sailing at Frensham Pond Sailing Club at the age of 10. Sixteen years later, she raced in the 2008 Olympic Games in China, having finished third at the Women's Laser Radial World Championships.

Andrea, how did you build a career that led to becoming a professional sailor?

It was just a natural progression. I was successful at junior and youth level, so the youth squad coach encouraged me to try Olympic sailing.

Compared to most people, you have a very unusual job. Can you explain what it entails?

I do lots of training, both on the water and in the gym, to prepare myself for competitions.

To retain my funding, I have to reach certain targets at either the Worlds or Europeans each year, so there is a clear incentive to perform. If you don't get the results, then the money stops, which can really put the pressure on.

We are all human and you are in a competitive profession. Do some racers take a serious dislike to their rivals?

The point of racing is to win, so there are always disagreements on the water, but they are usually resolved either out there or in the protest room.

Many people work 9-5 from Monday to Friday and take 4 weeks for holidays each year. How does your working life compare?

The main racing season runs from spring to late summer, so that period is usually taken up with events and travel. Late summer to early autumn is a good time to take a holiday, as there are fewer events. For autumn and winter, the main focus is usually on training and planning the following year's schedule.

Is travel a perk of the job?

Travelling around the world is a perk, although the actual travelling is not – time differences and jet lag can be tough to adapt to. Also, it's no fun being in a van for days when driving to and from events in Europe!

How much time do you actually spend sailing?

This year I have scheduled 58 days of racing and at least 97 days of training. The rest of the time is spent travelling, resting or planning and logistics.

To retain my funding, I have to reach certain targets at either the Worlds or Europeans each year, so there is a clear incentive to perform.

All in a day's work for Andrea, but she knows that payment is linked to performance round the track.

Where do your wages come from? Do you earn a good income or just enough to keep sailing?

I am supported by Skandia Team GBR and UK Sport, which provides a good income. The funding I receive is spent on equipment, travel, accommodation and entry fees etc, with a proportion that goes towards rent and food. It's enough to campaign my Radial and not go hungry!

What are the best and worst things about your kind of work?

The best things have to be success, travelling the world and doing a job that keeps me fit and healthy. The worst things have to be feeling physically and emotionally exhausted by it all.

Have you got it all worked out for the future?

My plan is to take life as it comes, because that's what I have always done.

The best things have to be success, travelling the world and doing a job that keeps me fit and healthy. The worst things have to be feeling physically and emotionally exhausted by it all.

What qualities are most required as a professional racer?

Motivation and a good work ethic.

Do you have some advice for any young person who would like to follow your kind of career?

Always be realistic and be prepared for failure, but never give up.

■ **www.skandiateamgbr.com**   ❖

OLYMPIC SAILOR – Paul Campbell-James

RYA Skandia GBR

Paul became a full time sailor in 2000. He started his most recent campaign with Mark Asquith in 2004, sailing a 49er with the RYA Olympic Squad.

Paul, how did you build a career that led to becoming a professional sailor?

I came up through the RYA youth program, starting in Optimists, moving on to 420's at the age of 15 and then match racing during university, before starting in the 49er. I studied Ship Science at uni, which was a back-up in case I didn't make it sailing, meaning I could always work in the industry.

Compared to many people, you have a very unusual job. Can you explain what it entails?

My average training day starts with an hour and a half run, then two sailing sessions of about 2-3 hours, followed by a debrief and any necessary work on the boat. A typical non-training day will have a longer gym session in the morning, after which we will be organising logistics for the next three months of events and training sessions.

I'm writing this from Miami in January, having flown here after two months in Australia. We are lucky enough to train in pretty warm locations all the way through the year! That's great, but it takes a lot of time making sure boats are in their container before you arrive some three months later, not to mention all the work that has to be done on flights, accommodation, visas, event entries and everything else.

We are all human and you are in a competitive profession. Do some racers take a serious dislike to their rivals?

Not so much in the 49er class, where everyone is pretty friendly. However, it's good to always have someone you're really gunning for within the fleet, which keeps you fired up!

Can you give a run-down on what happens during a typical working year?

A typical year starts with winter training in Australia during November and December, followed by Miami in January, then back to Europe for training at Palma de Mallorca during February, March and early April. The rest of the summer will be divided between all the European regattas, after which we normally get a bit of time off after the English event in September.

So as you can see, there's lots of travelling and not much of a routine. Some people wouldn't be able to deal with only spending three weeks at home between November and July and living out of a bag, but I haven't done a winter in the UK for about four years so I'm definitely not complaining!

Is travel a perk of the job?

Definitely for me, but plenty of sailors prefer to do as little as possible.

How much time do you actually spend sailing?

Between 3 and 6 hours, 5 days a week, depending on the wind conditions.

Where do your wages come from? Do you earn a good income or just enough to keep sailing? Do you ever worry about the future and how to pay the bills?

Our wages come from the national lottery funding. It's barely enough to keep sailing, so a few days of big boat sailing during off periods are normally required to pay the bills. The future will be fine as long as we achieve our goals. If we don't, I would be able to earn twice as much from professional yachting, so it doesn't worry me.

Presumably you are paid to perform. Does that put a lot of pressure on you? If you fail, does the money stop?

Yeah, if we don't make the cut (top 3, top 10 or top 20) at the World Championships we don't get any money – it's very black and white! The figures are insane when you think about the difference a few places can make in a race. But you'd go mental if you thought about it too much, so I'm pretty good at not thinking about things that I can't affect. For instance, in the last World Championships we missed a 50% pay rise, not to mention the sponsorship opportunities, by 3 points. However, if we'd missed the last race we would have got £0 for the next 18 months!

What are the best and worst things about your kind of work?

The best for me is that I'm sailing, which I love doing, in awesome countries around the world, against the best sailors in the world, improving all the time. Plus it's my job! The worst thing is the fact I'm barely earning anything and could lose my job, due to something out of my control, at any minute. For example, if the lottery funding gets used for something else or the 49er gets thrown out of the Olympics.

Have you got it all worked out for the future? Can you turn your career in alternative directions?

My long term plan is to go towards the America's Cup after winning a gold medal in the Olympics. At any point I could stop and go into boat design (or container ships if I've had enough of sailing!)

Training and racing are fundamentals to being an Olympic pro sailor.

What qualities are most required as a professional racer?

Being able to deal with pressure, work well as a team and the ability to stay calm.

Do you have some advice for any young person who would like to follow your kind of career?

You've really got to love doing it. You also need to sail with someone who you get on with very well!

■ www.skandiateamgbr.com ❖

PRO RACING CREW – David 'Freddie' Carr

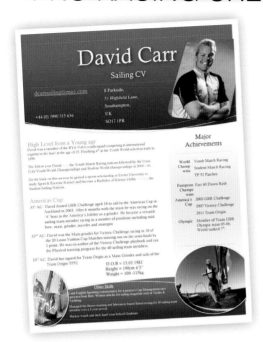

By the time he was twenty, David Carr has carved out a career as a professional crew, travelling the world to race thrilling boats at thrilling events. He explains what it takes to get there.

David, how did you build your career?

I started by landing on my feet at the age of 18, when I got the opportunity to work alongside the best sailors in Britain with the GBR Challenge Team. I saw what world class guys like Ado Stead, Chris Mason and James Stag did to be at the top of their game and have been trying to do the same ever since. One job led to another and by the age of 26 I found myself with a varied and successful sailing CV.

What have been your big breaks?

I was involved with the RYA youth squad systems in Lasers and as a youth match racer. In 2000 I got my first big break by winning the youth match racing worlds with James

Ward and Mark Campbell-James. Not long after, I found out that Ian Walker wanted some 'nippers' to help with GBR Challenge. So I went to help in the GBR Challenge loft and did all the worst jobs you can think of, but thanks to my size I got to grind on the boats as well. I have never learnt so much as in those first six months of 2001. It was the America's Cup Jubilee at the end of that summer, and when some of the older grinders were injured I got called up to race on the 'A boat' against Prada and Team New Zealand as an 18 year old! I worked hard, did a solid job and have never looked back.*

How important are qualifications, experience, contacts and pure luck in your profession?

All the above have played a part in my career. I do not have many RYA badges or certificates, but knew from an early age that I wanted to be a pro racer. There are not too many qualifications for that kind of career, but I think it is important to have a RIB driving qualification and be a trained first aider.

I worked hard at a young age to impress the right people when I was on a boat with them, and also gave 100% all the time I was racing. I have also learnt a lot from chatting with the older pros, as they have seen it all before and will point you in the right direction when you get to a crossroads in your sailing. For sure, I was lucky to get my first break with GBR Challenge and Ian Walker, which led to a high level of sailing. But after that first bit of luck it has all been down to hard work and learning every day I'm out on the water.

Not getting paid to sail as a young 'pro' is very common, but if you learn a lot it doesn't matter.

David (left) at work on Team Origin during the Louis Vuitton Pacific Series in Auckland, New Zealand.

Do you find the work or does the work find you?

Both. At a young age, I worked very hard on trying to get rides on boats where I could do important jobs like trimming or doing the pit. Not getting paid to sail as a young 'pro' is very common, but if you learn a lot it doesn't matter. As I got older, work began to come to me which was great – like getting hunted to lead the grinding team for Victory Challenge! But I would never get lazy and assume that will always be the case. When a great project came along like the Team Origin America's Cup challenge, I did everything possible to get an interview with Mike Sanderson.

Can you make a good living as a pro racer?

No question that when you are involved with an America's Cup or Volvo Ocean Race team, you can earn great money on a monthly salary for a long time. As an America's Cup sailor you earn every penny by working every hour God sends, but it's worth it to be part of the world's greatest sailing event. When I am not involved in a Cup cycle, piecing together three programmes over the year is really much harder work and involves a lot of time away from home. In good months the money may be better than a Cup salary, but you have to save for leaner times in the winter!

Following the America's Cup, what kind of boats did you work on?

During the 2008 season I combined working as a bowman on the Team Oman Extreme 40 in the iShares Cup, with working as a grinder on Rio Origin's TP52 and as an in-port race grinder on the Green Dragon Volvo 70. It meant I was travelling all over the place and spending a lot of time living out of suitcases.

...continued over

Sprinting across the trampoline of an Extreme 40 catamaran, racing in the iShares Cup, is all part of a day's work.

www.lloydimages.com

By the end of the year I was in Oman, helping to set up Oman Sail which aims to introduce sailing as the nation's number one sport, followed by more time in Oman for winter training. Jobs for 2009 included more racing in the iShares Cup, more time on board Rio Origin's TP52 in Miami and Key West, and more in-port grinding for Green Dragon during stop-overs on the Volvo Ocean Race. But when the America's Cup gets back on track, my hope is to be sailing in Team Origin's colours.

When do you get too old to be a professional racer? Can you turn your career in alternative directions?

I want to carry on sailing as a career until I stop improving within myself, stop getting rides on the good boats or simply lose the passion. I have always said that the day I come off the water and have not enjoyed it, because it felt like a job, I would stop. I have come close to losing that love, but deep down I am striving to achieve big things in the sport. However, if you are doing a physical job on the boat then age will one day catch up with you. Having said

As an America's Cup sailor you earn every penny by working every hour God sends, but it's worth it to be part of the world's greatest sailing event.

...that, Andrew Taylor is still one of the best grinders in the world, despite being well into his 40's, because he's looked after himself and his experience is second to none. I see myself sailing on race boats as long as I am good enough, which I hope is for a few more years yet, though I might need to change jobs on the boat to keep myself fresh. In the long term, I would love to be a sailing manager of a Cup team, but that is a while off yet.

What are the best parts of working as a pro racing crew? What are the worst parts?

Lining up against the best in the world and beating them! The day we beat Alinghi in Act 13 of the 32nd America's Cup was the best day on the water in my life. Worst part is not seeing my wife and family enough. Bianca (my wife) has known me since I was 17, so knew what she was getting involved in, but neither of us imagined I would be away as much as I have been over the last 8 years. I love living in England but never seem to be there!

Do things sometimes go awfully wrong when you are racing with a pro team?

Injuries are the worst. I have seen some nasty things happen that I would not wish on anyone. America's Cup boats and huge Maxis have massive loads and sometimes, no matter how good you are, things come unstuck. There is an element of risk. I have had a mainsheet turning block fire off past my leg and straight through the deck. If it had hit my leg, that would have been the end of my sailing!

Do professionals sometimes fall out with other members of the team or people who employ them?

I like to think of myself as the team clown, which helps me get on with most people. But you have to gauge where and when to have fun. As you live and work with your team mates, you have to learn when to have a bit of time apart. I get very good at reading people. If I have a run-in with another team member, I try to talk about it with them, there and then. Whatever happens, you must never let your personal feeling for someone get in the way of sailing at your highest level. It soon becomes very clear who you can have a pint with after racing, and they are the people you see time and time again on the circuit as they get on with people. The sailing world is too small to fall out!

What qualities and characteristics are most required as a pro racing crew?

Fitness is more important in sailing than most people realise. Think all the time about what will make the boat go faster or manoeuvre better. Work hard but have fun. Write everything you learn down – I have notes that are my life blood.

Can you give some tips for people who would like to follow your kind of career?

Have your own style of doing things, but be open to learn from others every time you get on the water. Be confident in your own skills, but adapt to every boat that you sail on. The day you stop enjoying sailing, STOP!

It is my passion before it is my job. ❖

Working as a coach requires dedication, inspiration and communication to enhance sailing skills...

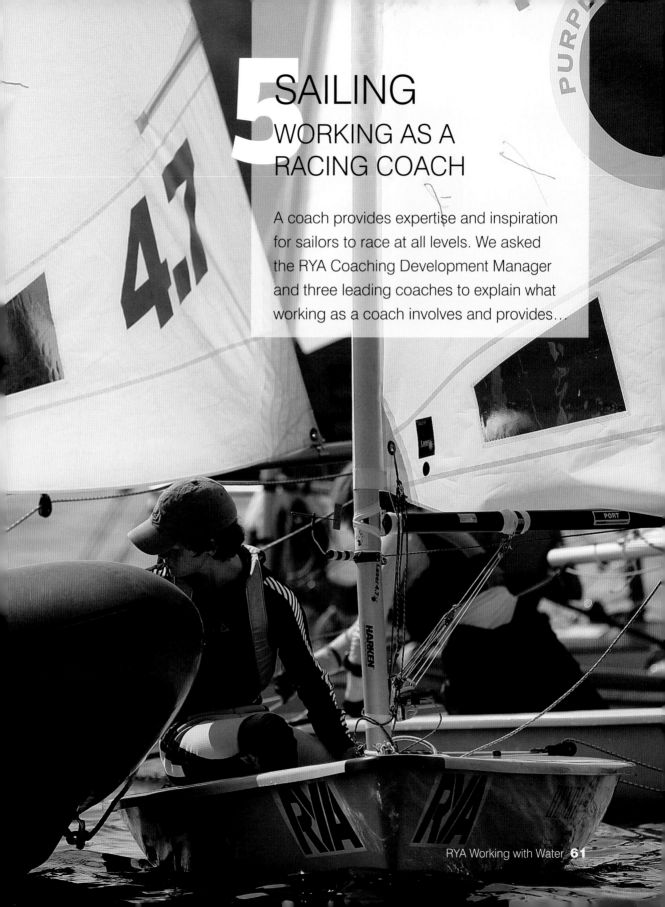

5 SAILING
WORKING AS A RACING COACH

A coach provides expertise and inspiration for sailors to race at all levels. We asked the RYA Coaching Development Manager and three leading coaches to explain what working as a coach involves and provides…

RYA COACHING DEVELOPMENT MANAGER – Helen Cartwright

RYA

Helen, can you explain the difference between a sailing instructor and a coach?

An instructor tells the pupil what to do – for instance, "Pull the tiller towards you!" A coach uses feedback to achieve the desired results – for instance, "What does it feel like if you pull the tiller towards you?"

How did you career develop?

Until the age of 20, I was a full time sailor on the RYA World Class Program competing in the Mistral Olympic Class. I had taken my instructor's qualification and worked at my local sailing centre teaching windsurfing, whenever I had free time. I also took four A Levels and went to John Moores University in Liverpool to study Applied Sports Performance (BSc Hons). During this time I was asked to coach the West Zone Squad, which provided a very fast learning curve in coaching young sailors. I was then asked to coach a Junior National Squad on an overseas training camp to Israel, and the following year

was appointed as RYA National Junior Coach for windsurfers.

The post of RYA National Windsurfing Coach came up while I was in the last year of my degree. This job really interested me, as it included both coaching on the ground and strategic management, allowing me to grow my ideas and develop the sport. I remained in this position for seven years, coaching the Olympic Women's Performance Squad, Youth Sailors and Olympic Development Sailors. In 2008 I applied for the post of RYA Coaching Development Manager, providing education and development opportunities for sailing coaches.

What does your job at the RYA involve?

I have to ensure that coaches are educated, qualified and supported in delivering World Class Coaching, from grass roots to elite level. My team includes a Coaching Development Officer and two administrators who are crucial to the smooth running of the coach development team. They have responsibility for booking courses, taking in course results and supporting coaches in achieving their action plans. They also keep our coaches up to date and validated in terms of first aid and power boating. The Coach Development Officer manages and leads the grassroots side of Coach Development, ensuring that volunteers and coaches working in hundreds of clubs and centres around the UK are supported and supplied with the highest possible levels of information and learning.

What kind of experience and temperament are required to work as a coach?

To work on RYA Programs as a coach, you must have a minimum of RYA Racing Coach Level 2.

There is no getting away from the fact that sailing is an experience based sport, so it is very unlikely that you would be able to provide world class coaching to an elite sailor if you had only sailed at a low level. However, one of the most important factors of coaching is the ability to be flexible – to change your style and approach with regards to whom, why and where you are coaching. It is a dynamic job and for the majority of the time you are working on your own initiative.

The best aspects of working as a professional coach are being able to devote time, effort and passion to the cause, to be in a position where you leave no stone unturned and get things right rather than 'making do'. This is when results and progress occur and the job is fantastic. The worst aspect has to be packing up the coach boat at the end of a long, cold, winter day, when it is normally dark and raining!

What kind of opportunities are available for working as a coach?

There are many job opportunities for talented coaches and we are always searching for good coaches to keep the RYA programs moving forwards. A good coach can be in very high demand. Many of our coaches work full time and earn decent salaries, with the added benefit of being self employed and flexible. Some coaches do other work, especially at a Zone and Junior level where coaching only takes place during sailors' weekends or school holidays. Coaches

progress by showing they are committed, hard working and willing to continually develop their own ability. This is only possible if you truly enjoy and have a passion for sailing and supporting those who learn.

Presumably some professional coaches are ranked as leaders in their field. What sets them apart?

Some coaches are in more demand than others, normally due to the fact that they are reliable, thorough, have good self initiative and are deemed 'a safe pair of hands'! You also cannot get away from the fact that coaches with huge experience and skill at delivering their knowledge are highly valuable.

What advice would you give to a young person who is coming up to leaving school and is interested in working as a coach?

Shadow other coaches, involve yourself in as much coaching as possible (even as a volunteer) and find ways to develop your own learning.

Any advice you would like to add?

You have to love coaching to live with coaching in the long run. It is a hard job, challenging, frustrating and at times lonely, but when it goes right the rewards are massive and it is the best job in the world. ❖

A good coach can be in very high demand. Many of our coaches work full time and earn decent salaries, with the added benefit of being self employed and flexible.

RYA Skandia GBR

TOP OLYMPIC COACH – Chris Gowers

RYA Skandia GBR

Who do you work for?

I am self-employed, but a large part of my work is for 'Sparky', the Olympic Manager and Barrie Edgington, the Olympic Development Squads Manager, who are both at the RYA. I also do some work for sailing clubs, a little Optimist coaching in Wales and other bits and pieces where necessary.

Can you summarise what your job involves?

The simple answer is no! Each job has different goals and responsibilities, but common threads are assessing the needs of a group of sailors and then helping them achieve their goals, drawing on my own experience and knowledge and other specialists where required. It's a lot simpler when those goals, and particularly the achievement, match those of the person who is paying the bills!

Chris, how did you build a career as a coach? Was it an accident, or did you plan things that way?

I trained as a teacher, but early on it was apparent that coaching sailing was what I found most satisfying – apart from campaigning! When lottery funding started, it was obvious there were going to be more opportunities and only then did I start believing it was a career option. I still don't know what I want to do when I grow up!

What was your training?

A degree in PE and Sports Science, a Post Graduate Certificate of Education, more years than I care to count campaigning, five years at the National Watersports Centre for Wales (Plas Menai) and working alongside the likes of Jim Saltonstall were all fundamental building blocks for the work I do today.

I presume it's not 9-5. Can you give us an idea of a working year?

As far as the Olympic cycle goes it's 9-5, starting at 0900 yesterday and finishing at approx 1700 on 8th Aug 2012, if all goes to plan! With the ISAF World Cup in the northern hemisphere there is a rhythm to the year, which might become more of a fixed routine. Winter and spring are spent supporting the performance sailors on and off the water. Regatta support becomes a larger emphasis as the European circuit gets underway, the results of which lead to some tweaking and adjustments on the training plan. The end of summer usually requires a peak for the sailors where results really matter, followed by the autumn when there is a bit of a break, providing time for a review of the season and confirming plans for the next year.

Chris at work during the French Olympic Sailing Week at Hyeres. Communication, insight and RIB handling skills are all part of the job.

Most Junior and Youth work tends be done during the winter and prevents things getting too quiet. Other work fits when possible and where needed. If I'm away at training camps or regattas, any schedule needs to be pretty flexible – we all know our sport relies on the weather, which doesn't have great timekeeping!

Does your work involve a jet set lifestyle?

Once the season starts travel is pretty much non-stop. Fortunately, shipping boats around the world isn't a pre-requisite for the Laser class, but getting home for more than a few days a month is rare. Sometimes it's easy to moan, but without it I'm sure I would be complaining of boredom! I've had the opportunity to visit cities and countries I could never afford if I was paying for the flights. I particularly look forward to tapas and Rioja in Palma each March, but we're there to do a job, so getting on the water and moving any program forward is always the highlight. Pwllheli in February might not fit the 'jet set' title but can

provide the odd wonderful day where the sun is reflecting off the snow on Snowdon, there's a large swell from south and the juniors are yee-haaing their way back to the beach!

What qualities and characteristics are required for your job?

Water resistance! At different times you need to be able to draw on a variety of skills and styles, sometimes against your natural inclination. Perversely, patience becomes more important as you work with more skilful sailors, since minute improvements are only apparent over a season or two. Working with relative novices can be much more motivating as you can see the improvements week on week. It's becoming a bit of a worn-out mantra at the RYA, but I believe 'fascination with the process' is the most important characteristic. Without it you will struggle to keep motivated, whilst exploring avenues that might eventually prove to be dead ends. ...continued over...

Blue sky is a bonus when Chris is cleaning up and packing up at the end of a coaching session.

What are the best and worst parts of your job?

The best are being out on the water and helping to change behaviour. The worst are packing containers in 40 degrees C and high humidity, seeing the same mistakes again and again, long postponements and hail!

What are your objectives for the future? Can you turn your sailing career in alternative directions?

That would be telling! Recently sailing coaches from the UK have become a business coach, manager of the Olympic Regatta 2012, unemployed and sailing coaches for the enemy. A number of the skills you learn and practise as a coach are transferable, but once addicted it's hard to give up. You just become wiser, but physically less able to do the job!

What are the main differences between coaching sailors at Olympic level and coaching sailors at lower levels?

The key is that the more experienced a sailor is, the more they lead and own the program. Hopefully they will heed your advice – that's why they work with you. At lower levels, you might be able to convince the sailors that it's 'their program' but you really need to lead – after all, you are the 'expert'.

Can you give some tips for people who would like to follow your kind of career?

Attend an RYA Level 2 coaching course. Research coaching theory, but take it all with an open mind and a pinch of salt. Assist experienced coaches at any level, but youth to development squad level might be most enlightening. Get out on the water and run sessions at your local club, review your 'performance' and finally heed a quote from my first boss Bob Bond – "If your students are acting like turkeys, get your feathers on!" ❖

OLYMPIC SQUAD COACH – Steve Lovegrove

RYA Skandia GBR

Hi Steve, how did you build your career?

After spending all my working life in and around the marine trade and campaigning 470 and Tornado Olympic classes, I became fascinated with ways of enhancing performance when I stopped competing at the end of 2002. I worked in a variety of other sports before returning to sailing, starting as a private coach to Paul Brotherton and Mark Asquith in their campaign for selection to the 2004 Olympics. That led to working with the RYA as Tornado Development Squad coach and Women's 470 Squad coach.

Can you summarise what your job involves and how it takes you through the year?

My role as a squad coach is controlled by the amount of contact days the budget allows, which right now is about 150 days a year. The cycle of planning and review is ongoing, but assume a start date of Jan 1st when we highlight particular events for the year and define if they are 'outcome orientated' or events where a team may prioritise particular areas to work on or equipment to test. Additional non-event training will be planned around these key events.

We then determine how these events will fit into any technical development plans and what specialists we may want to include at events or squad training. Each team in the squad is responsible for their own logistical planning, although we liaise with the racing division at the RYA when longer distance shipment of boats is required. We endeavour to organise travel plans well in advance to save vital resources.

Presumably, an important requirement for a top coach is personal ability to race at top level. What other qualities and characteristics are required?

I'm not convinced that racing at top level is a requirement for top coaches, although I do believe a very keen ability to identify differences in set-up and techniques is crucial. Being able to relate to the individual needs of the sailors and having the skill to discuss, identify and communicate a variety of potential solutions are far more important than personal racing experience.

Being able to relate to the individual needs of the sailors and having the skill to discuss, identify and communicate a variety of potential solutions are far more important than personal racing experience.

A normal working day for Steve – coaching 470 girls off Weymouth, site of the 2012 Olympic Sailing event.

RYA Skandia GBR

Do you need experience of every type of boat you coach for, or are many elements of coaching the same, regardless of the class?

Essentially we coach people, not sailing. All the sailors operating at the level I coach will already possess most of the skills they require to compete at a top level. Being able to identify tiny areas where improvements may be made is more important than a specific knowledge of the class. However, some sailors will gain initial confidence in a coach they perceive as having first-hand knowledge of a class. So we always have the option of bringing in a particular expert when a squad coach may not possess all the information.

What are the best and worst parts of your job?

Best is seeing teams I coach becoming more professional, focused athletes, identifying and developing skills they need to be world class sailors. Worst is extracting a RIB from the back of the RYA compound on a dark morning in February.

Do what you love and love what you do. It's a cliché, but if you start thinking about what you get paid each hour everything will go downhill.

What are your objectives for the future?

Develop the current squad to be a dominant force in women's 470 sailing in the run-up to the Weymouth Olympics and also for 2016. For the time being that's enough!

Can you give some tips for people who would like to follow your kind of career?

Do what you love and love what you do. It's a cliché, but if you start thinking about what you get paid each hour everything will go downhill. Have fun and don't compromise, because you wouldn't expect your sailors to! Always set a good example – it's the very best way of influencing people. ❖

JUNIOR COACH & OSTEOPATH
– Kirsty Bonar

Kirsty, how did you become a Junior Coach? Was it an accident, or did you plan things that way?

I sailed a full Olympic campaign in the Europe for the Athens Games. This unfortunately came to a premature end as I tore my knee ligaments in a fall. Over the campaign, I worked as a sailing instructor and began to get involved in junior coaching with the Optimist National Squad and headed up the Topper East Zone Squad. Initially, this was a way of funding my campaign, but very quickly it became a great hobby where I could spend my time with motivated youngsters and watch them develop.

When my full time sailing stopped abruptly, I became more involved in coaching as it allowed me to make kids enjoy their racing and achieve or often exceed their potential. It's great to see so many now involved in Olympic campaigns, but it does make me feel a little old! I also wanted to resume my medical career, which had been put on hold by sailing full time. So

I embarked on a four-year course to become an osteopath, while heading up the Laser 4.7 National Squad and still involved with Optimists.

Do you regard coaching as part of your working life?

Now that I've qualified, my working life is very much a mix of fixing people and coaching. I coach most weekends of the year with the Lasers and Optimists and also take them out to international events such as the Laser Worlds and Europeans in Croatia, Brazil and Finland and Optimist Europeans in Italy and Slovenia, which is nice! It provides a useful income, but for the hours involved in travelling, preparation and long days it's really more for love!

I also find that when I'm coaching I see life through the eyes of an osteopath. This allows some extra input on areas such as hiking techniques or fitness and I often end up assessing niggles, injuries and answering questions that kids or their parents may have about growing pains. Always on duty really!

What are the best and worst parts of working as a coach?

Best are really all of the above, or I wouldn't do it! I love the interaction with kids. The pressures are only just starting at junior level and so the emphasis is on fun, challenge and achieving as much as possible. The other junior coaches are great – a constant source of inspiration and great ideas when we meet up, in order to keep sessions interesting and fun for the kids. We have a very good programme of coaching development and are kept well up to date with new thoughts, techniques and knowledge.

I also love the foreign travel to international events and the challenges that go hand in hand with new situations and guiding kids.

RYA

**Coaching can be as much or little as you want it to be.
I decided I didn't want coaching as a full time job…**

The worst bits are probably travelling. The novelty of hours and hours on the motorway each Friday and Sunday night soon wears off and your social life takes a dive! But lots of fellow coaches become very good friends, so it's great to see them at the weekend.

What qualities and characteristics are required to coach young people?

A sense of humour! Things don't always go according to plan, so the ability to laugh is key! Commitment to a program is a significant investment of time and energy. I guess you need to be quite selfless, as the process is about making others achieve. Coaching also develops your ability to talk in front of people and put together structured plans. A fascination with the processes is necessary. Sometimes, potential gains that make all the difference are very small, so you're like a detective a lot of the time. Basic requirements such as First Aid, radio use and
safety afloat always need updating. Above all, you have to enjoy it!

Could you turn your coaching into a full time career?

Coaching can be as much or little as you want it to be. I decided I didn't want coaching as a full time job, as I wanted to have a career in another area, whilst always being keen to coach at weekends. To keep coaching fresh, you need to keep challenging yourself and always get fully involved. There's nothing better than a coach who works as hard as the kids!

Can you give some final tips for people who would like to try working as a coach?

Go for it and try it. Volunteer and get as much exposure as you can to different levels from beginner to advanced, since all experience is good experience. Assist, gain confidence and keep enjoying. ❖

RYA RACING COACH QUALIFICATIONS

Level 2 Coach
Minimum age: 16.

■ **Requirements:** Good club racer with appropriate racing knowledge; RYA Powerboat Level 2 certificate; RYA recommended First Aid certificate.

■ **Useful qualifications:** Previous instructing experience. Qualified to teach Level 4 'Start Racing' and 'Intermediate Racing' at a Race Training Centre or RYA affiliated club, with the object of introducing novices to racing and facilitating race training. The course length is one weekend run at local clubs and administered by the RYA Coaching Development Team. Variations on the course specialise in Team Racing and Keelboat Racing coaches, as well as Junior and Youth Coaches who are often ex-youth squad sailors.

Level 3 Coach
Minimum age: 18.

■ **Requirements:** Top 20% of class; Level 2 Racing Coach with one year's experience; to have assisted a Level 3 Racing Coach or RYA Squad Training; recommended by class or High Performance Manager/National Coach.

■ **Useful qualifications:** Previous instructing experience. Qualified to teach all racing schemes, with the object of improving the standard of race training at class level or within an RYA Squad. The course length is two weekends of theory and practical, plus one weekend's assessment with a National Coach.

Jeremy Evans

WINDSURFING
WORKING AS AN INSTRUCTOR

6

Would you like to teach windsurfing, with free access to great equipment and the possibility of being based in a superb high wind location? The opportunities are ready and waiting…

Neilson

AMANDA VAN SANTEN
– RYA CHIEF WINDSURFING INSTRUCTOR

RYA

Amanda, can you tell us how your career developed?

I have always been a keen water person, so when I heard about intensive instructor courses (better known as 'zero to hero') I took the leap and signed on at an RYA centre in Cornwall. We covered a variety of sports – windsurfing, dinghy sailing, kayaking and surf life saving – taking you from no experience to an instructor course. It was hard work and needed a lot of dedication, but the rewards I would gain later made it all worthwhile. I actually never intended to be in the industry full time – I just thought it would be a stop gap.

On completing the course, the centre

asked me to stay and work for the season. I still remember the sessions I ran as if it was yesterday. The butterflies were incredible, but taking someone from complete beginner to being able to complete basic skills, like sailing across the wind and back, was such a fantastic feeling. I was definitely addicted.

I spent the next years upping my skills, windsurfing as much as possible and working at a variety of RYA Training Centres in the UK and overseas, ranging from small centres struggling to break even to large commercial operations. Seasons like that are hard work but so rewarding – it's a great way to gain as much experience as possible.

After I had been working overseas, I decided to challenge myself further. I had always admired the people who ran my instructor courses and dreamt that one day I could also pass my knowledge to potential instructors. So I returned to the UK and started my progression to become an RYA Trainer, which I finally gained in 2004. Everything came together while I was working for an RYA centre on the Isle of Wight. They asked me to run their instructor training in Australia, and while over there I heard about the job opportunity as Chief Windsurfing Instructor at the RYA. I thought, "That's where I want to be, in charge of running the training schemes". I guess the rest is history – here I am in the position I always wanted to hold!

What does your job at the RYA involve?

Chief Instructors work within the Training Department at the RYA, looking after specific training schemes. For me this is windsurfing and currently involves about 260 Windsurfing Training Centres in the UK and overseas, 2,200 instructors and 70 trainers who deliver instructor training, as well as our trained inspectors who help with the annual inspection of Training Centres.

My responsibilities include ensuring that the windsurfing scheme is accessible to the participant, instructor and centre. This is carried out via the National and Youth Windsurfing Scheme, by making sure they are up to date and meeting the needs of beginners and progressing windsurfers. RYA Training, along with the Publications Department, produces an array of training publications complementing our schemes or individual course. My role is to revise and technically edit publications such as scheme logbooks and handbooks. We also work closely with other departments, such as Sports Development, on initiatives to encourage people into the sport.

What kind of experience and temperament are required to work as a windsurfing instructor?

Patience and lots of it! For me, it was important that I enjoyed teaching people of any level, helping them progress in the sport of windsurfing. I always thought I should stop if this ever disappeared, but it never went away. My love for the sports I was teaching and being outdoors were always an asset. This industry can bring such variety – one day you will be teaching beginners in a Force 2 with beautiful sunshine, the next it could be raining with gale force winds on the way.

Becoming an instructor is where the RYA schemes are world leaders. By following the RYA training courses, I could plan my journey to become an instructor. It was very clear what level I needed to attain and any additional courses I needed to take, such as First Aid or Powerboat Level 2. Each scheme is progressive, so you know exactly what should come next. The RYA Training Website (www.ryatraining.co.uk) provides lots of information on course pre-requisites and when and where they are being run.

Being dual-qualified definitely helped me in the industry, not only with getting jobs but also having a broad knowledge of what is going on.

What kind of job opportunities are available for people who want to work as windsurfing instructors?

The opportunities are as big or as small as you want to make them. Looking for gap year or summer work? Summer time is usually one of the busiest times for our centres, therefore students with instructional qualifications can find some great working opportunities at a variety of locations.

Being dual-qualified definitely helped me in the industry, not only with getting jobs but also having a broad knowledge of what is going on. Many of our training centres offer windsurfing and dinghy sailing, so it may well be an advantage if you have both qualifications, instead of just teaching one sport. For those who want to make a full time career in this industry, the RYA sets out clear instructional pathways and qualifications. My chosen qualifications and pathway reflect the fact that all I wanted to do was Instructor Training. Others may choose to work towards running a club, local council centre, large commercial operation or working with disadvantaged groups, or why not a mixture of them all!

What advice would you give to a young person who is coming up to leaving school and wants to work and windsurf at the same time?

This is where I really did make the most of qualifications and potential opportunities. The RYA has training centres all over the world, but some of the best locations are in the UK. Take the first steps and become an instructor. Speak to centres about jobs as early as possible. You will normally have to work a few seasons as a basic instructor before being offered the more senior positions, or more desirable windier locations if working overseas. My advice would be to stick with it and keep progressing at your coaching, qualifications or management skills. Doors will start to open and provide some great opportunities.

I took up windsurfing comparatively late. As I progressed and became more addicted, I wanted to get more and more time on the water. During my first few seasons I concentrated on my instructor qualifications and ensured I progressed as much as possible, choosing centres that would enable me to become the best coach possible. I looked for centres that

worked the conventional season from April to October, with locations that were not necessarily the windiest, but provided some great coaching opportunities and enabled me to save as much money as possible. So then I could take the winter off and go windsurfing, enjoying the best of both worlds. I did this for a number of years, sailing and teaching in some of the most amazing places – for instance working for the UKSA provided me with a great job and some amazingly challenging sailing spots on opposite sides of the world.

What are the best and worst elements of working as a windsurfing instructor?

Imagine being paid to do a job you love, which is also your hobby, usually in some of the most breathtaking places! But as with all jobs there are bad days. Being an instructor or running a centre is hard work with long hours and potentially variable weather conditions, while friends are tucked up in their cosy offices. But if you ask most instructors, any bad memories seem to dissolve quickly and a Cheshire cat of a grin appears as they reflect on seasons past!

Do you ever get situations where potential windsurfing instructors fail to match the required standards?

It is possible to not meet the required standards to become an instructor, but rare. Our trainers do a fantastic job in getting candidates to the required level, but if the candidate is not willing to commit and complete the work required, they may not succeed. Action plans can be put together for candidates who need a little extra time or help.

Any advice you would like to add?

The watersports industry can provide enormous opportunities if you wish to find them. But it's not for lazy people – you need to be committed and ready for hard work! ❖

WINDSURFING MANAGER – Jono Dunnett

Minorca Sailing

Ten years ago, Jono Dunnett got a job as an instructor with Minorca Sailing Holidays, thought it was nicer than Clacton and decided to make his home on the island where he works as Windsurfing Beach Manager.

Instructors…

We usually need 4 or 5 five windsurfing instructors, with double the number in peak season. Most recruitment is over the winter, which gives a chance to meet people face to face for an interview. An informative and professionally presented CV is essential. We are looking for motivated instructors with good communication skills and a genuine enthusiasm for teaching. A high personal standard of windsurfing is useful, but the type of person is more important. The RYA qualification is important to get a job, but ability and experience dictate the type of instructing you will do. When you've worked a few seasons, pay is more closely linked to experience than qualifications.

A typical working day…

Open the centre in the morning and sort out any problems with kit. Prepare the morning session for your group who will arrive at 10:00am. Have a cracking session where your group progress in leaps and bounds and become hooked on the sport. Go windsurfing during your lunch hour. The day's second session is more of the same or something different – being adaptable is important – which may include one-on-one taster sessions in light afternoon winds. Close the school and catch up on that skipped lunch. Head out with other instructors for a quiet cerveza before an early night, ready for the next day…

■ www.minorcasailing.co.uk   ❖

WORKING AT A BEACH CLUB – Simon Davis

Neilson

Simon Davis is Overseas Operations Manager for Neilson, with responsibility for 10 bases.

Hi Simon, could you give some background?

I am 35 years old, and have been a windsurfing trainer for nine years. I started work as an RYA windsurfing instructor when I was 16, did some summer seasons at Bray Watersports and then went to work for Neilson overseas as a Senior Instructor and eventually Resort Manager. I came back to work at Neilson's UK base ten years ago and became Overseas Operations Manager, looking after the delivery of all our summer beach and yachting holidays on the activity side. We have ten bases in Europe and Turkey, which I visit on a regular basis to support our resort managers.

How many windsurfing instructors do Neilson employ during the season?

We employ around 200 instructors. Many hold both dinghy and windsurfing qualifications, as most of our resorts deliver both activities.

How do you find new instructors?

We seem to be in the fortunate position that they find us. Our staff make our holidays a success, so we try to provide our instructors with the best possible package, including training. Many of our instructors return year after year and progress into different roles. They are a great team who do us credit – we get that feedback from customers on a regular basis.

What qualities are you looking for when you employ instructors?

Neilson is very focused on our customers' experience, and we expect our staff to think the same way. We need team players who have the ability to develop what we offer, can make positive input and are excited by the opportunity to work in an environment that treats them with value.

Are qualifications, ability or experience more important?

An RYA instructor's qualification will always get everyone off to a good start in the application process. If they have come through the scheme, it shows that a candidate has learnt the right way to teach others well. That said, we will also take people on who have just the right approach to their work – the kind of people who you know will just fit. We have a certain number of assistant roles available, where we will train them over the summer and put them through the instructor course at the end of the season. With only ten slots available they can be sought after!

What's the pay like? Is it linked to qualifications and experience?

Travel, food and accommodation are provided. We also have a bursary scheme to financially help all staff with any qualification that will help push our service forward.

The higher your qualifications the more you are able to earn, and also there is the opportunity to progress to a supervisor or management role.

Is it possible to save money while working on the beach?

Always – just depends on how much you spend!

How many hours do instructors have to work?

Day starts at between 8.30 and 9 to meet the team and get the beach set up. Courses start at 10 through to about 1pm, then start up again at around 2/2.30 and finish at about 4.30, eventually packing up the beach for about 6'ish – our customers can stay on the water until the last person comes off, but dinner tends to mean that most are in by 6.30 latest. Sometimes, you will be involved in an evening social event once or twice a week.

Our team get a day off each week and earn 2 days per month as holiday, which is generally saved to take a week off to go and explore the country they are working in.

What are the best things about working for Neilson? Are there perks, such as great equipment and great conditions? Are there drawbacks people should consider?

Equipment and conditions go without saying, but the best perk is really being in an environment with like-minded people, sharing experiences and meeting new friends. There are not many jobs where you have a raft of new faces turning up on a weekly basis, all of whom want to get better at an activity and have a great time on and off the water. The main point to consider is that working overseas is not about being either at work or not at work. It's not the kind of job you

clock in and out of and you don't get loads of time to yourself. If you like loads of your own time and space, then there are better jobs for you!

How much variety can instructors expect when working through the season?

As much as they want really – we want all of our team to teach a lot! That way they finish the season ready to move onto the next stage. We offer loads of activities other than windsurfing, so there is lots to learn if you want to get involved.

What are the prospects if an instructor wants to continue working with Neilson?

All of our Resort Managers and Supervisors have been developed within Neilson. Our Managing Director and Overseas Director started work as instructors with Neilson, when fluorescent shorts were in fashion the first time round! The guy researching new locations worked as a manager in the Caribbean for Neilson, our head of IT was a dinghy instructor and our Management Information Analyst was a bike guide. So there are prospects for moving on, though the number of vacancies will obviously be limited.

Do you have any gems of advice for newcomers who want to work on water?

Get your training in with the RYA. Most employers want to see that you have had a structured approach to training and teaching before even giving you an interview. Always remember why you gained the qualification – it's not just about making yourself better, but others as well. All of our team wants to excel at this, and a majority of them do.

■ **www.neilson.co.uk**   ❖

… the best perk is really being in an environment with like minded people, sharing experiences and meeting new friends

TOM BUGGY
GOOD TIMES AS A WINDSURFING INSTRUCTOR

Hi Tom, how many different places have you worked as a windsurfing instructor?

When I worked for the UKSA, I was based in Cowes and Australia for four years and finished off working in Dahab. Over the years I have also worked for Minorca Sailing Holidays, Outdoor Adventure, Sunsail and Pelican Point in Western Australia. I've been lucky enough to experience different centres around the world, filling my winters and other normally quiet times by working at faraway resorts.

How did you find work? What have been the highlights and major breaks?

All my jobs have been through word of mouth and getting to know the right people. Teaching for a season in western Oz was the best ever experience, because of the amazing conditions only a short drive from Perth. I also had an amazing four winters in Queensland in Australia.

The windsurfing was not world class, but the lifestyle was great! I could stay fit at the surf club and go surfing every day and when the wind blew we windsurfed until it got dark. Minorca Sailing always has the most amazing equipment, which enables you to get on the water in almost any kind of wind and have a blast.

What would you rate as the world's best places to work?

Hard to say as some places are excellent for teaching, but not always great for your own sailing. Swan River in Perth is a perfect beginner windsurfing spot, but on your day off you can drive for an hour to find windy, half mast height, cross shore perfection! Egypt is also good for teaching and personal sailing, but can be tricky with complete beginners due to the offshore winds.

Have you had any bad experiences?

Luckily, not too many to date apart from sitting around waiting for wind for days on end, which meant teaching wind and tide theory until I lost my voice.

Is there a big difference between working for different employers?

All places have their own standard operating procedures, which rubs off on the staff and management. But most people are in the industry because they love being on the water, so we always have something in common.

All my jobs have been through word of mouth and getting to know the right people. Teaching for a season in western Oz was the best ever experience…

The more qualifications you have, the more choice you get when it comes to working overseas. Also, you won't get bored doing the same thing day in day out.

Can you earn good enough money as an instructor?

When I left UKSA, I was earning about as much as you possibly can as an instructor, without ending up in the office running the day to day activities. If you are self-employed you can earn good money, but need to look for work. I made the natural progression to yacht skippering and racing, so I could earn more money on the water and spend it all on going windsurfing.

What advice would you give to a young person who wants to work on the water?

Try working at an RYA training centre so you can train while you work. The more qualifications you have, the more choice you get when it comes to working overseas. Also, you won't get bored doing the same thing day in day out.

How has your own career turned out?

You never know what lies around the corner. I had a good eight years teaching sailing, windsurfing and power-boating, clocking over 10,000 hours as an instructor. You can always develop your skills to run a centre or become a chief instructor, but I progressed to professional sailing on racing yachts, because the money is better and I get free weekends and evenings to sail or surf.

Any regrets?

None! I have had the most unbelievable lifestyle and fun doing my work and loved every minute of it. ❖

Windsurfing Assistant Instructor
Minimum Age: 14

■ **Essential requirements:** Recommended by RYA Principal; RYA Windsurfing Scheme intermediate non-planing certificate.

■ **Useful qualifications:** First Aid certificate; SRC radio certificate.

An Assistant Instructor is qualified to assist windsurfing instructors in teaching up to the standard of Youth Stage 1 and adult Start Windsurfing courses, under the supervision of a Senior Instructor. Training and assessment are conducted by the principal or chief instructor of a training centre who will award AI certificates, which are valid at that centre for 5 years. Training is based on RYA teaching methods for beginners and takes approximately 20 hours or 2 days.

Start Windsurfing Instructor
Minimum Age: 16

■ **Essential requirements:** First Aid certificate; RYA Powerboat Level 2 certificate; RYA Windsurfing Scheme intermediate non-planing certificate.

■ **Useful qualifications:** SRC radio certificate; RYA Safety Boat certificate.

RYA Start Windsurfing instructors are qualified to teach the Start Windsurfing course and Stages 1 and 2 of the Youth Windsurfing Scheme under the supervision of a senior instructor. The course lasts a full five days with continuous assessment, teaching candidates how to run on-water sessions and deliver shore-based talks.

Intermediate Windsurfing Instructor
Minimum Age: 16

■ **Essential requirements:** First Aid certificate; RYA Powerboat Level 2 certificate; 50 hours logged as Start Windsurfing Instructor. Intermediate non-planing instructors require RYA Windsurfing Scheme intermediate certificate, with beach start and non-planing carve gybe clinics. Intermediate planing instructors require RYA Windsurfing Scheme advanced certificate, with waterstart beach start and carve gybe clinics.

■ **Useful qualifications:** SRC radio certificate; RYA Safety Boat certificate.

RYA Intermediate Windsurfing instructors are qualified to teach the Intermediate course and Youth Windsurfing Scheme under the supervision of a senior instructor. The course lasts a full five days with continuous assessment in how to instruct non-planing or planing skills.

Vital Reading:
RYA Windsurfing
Instructor Manual

Minorca Sailing

Instructors at Minorca Sailing enjoy a blast.

Advanced Windsurfing Instructor

Minimum Age: 18

■ **Essential requirements:** First Aid certificate; RYA Powerboat Level 2 certificate; 100 hours logged as Intermediate Planing Instructor; minimum of very competent advanced certificate, with clinics on waterstarting and carve gybing.

■ **Useful qualifications:** SRC radio certificate; RYA Safety Boat certificate.

RYA Advanced Windsurfing instructors are qualified to teach the advanced course and all stages of the Youth Windsurfing Scheme under the supervision of a senior instructor. The course lasts a full five days with a clinic-based approach and continuous assessment.

Senior Windsurfing Instructor

Minimum Age: 18

■ **Essential requirements:** Recommended by RYA Principal; First Aid certificate; RYA Safety Boat certificate; two seasons full time as Start Windsurfing instructor.

■ **Useful qualifications: SRC radio certificate.**

RYA Senior Windsurfing instructors are qualified to organise and manage courses within the RYA Windsurfing Scheme, which includes supervising and assisting instructors. The course lasts a full four days. Windsurfing ability to at least RYA Intermediate non-planing instructor standard is required. An RYA recognised training centre must have an SI as its principal or chief instructor.

"Aaaargh! We can't stand them anymore! The lead boat crew decide to jump and swim"…

Sunsail

YACHT FLOTILLAS 7

Flotillas provide the opportunity to work and live afloat, escorting a small fleet of yachts around beautiful sailing areas. Most yacht flotillas operate on the Mediterranean coasts of Croatia, Greece and Turkey between April and October, while a few operate in popular cruising areas of the Caribbean such as the British Virgin Islands throughout the year. The work is interesting, but carries a lot of responsibility and can be tough.

FLOTILLA SKIPPER – Alex Evans

The skipper has total responsibilty for ensuring the flotilla moves safely from port to port, while clients enjoy their cruise to the maximum. This is a tough job that requires excellent social skills and the ability to inspire confidence throughout the flotilla, particularly if sailing conditions become difficult. Alex Evans has worked as a flotilla skipper and yacht manager for Neilson for several years, as well as being an RNLI crew back home in the UK.

Alex, can you give us some background on your career?

I've been around boats ever since I was a child. My father was a lifeboat man, as was my grandfather and uncle, so I spent most of my childhood weekends in and around the lifeboat station at Porthcawl. Many of the crew had boats and I learned to sail in an Oppie. For many years after that, a friend and myself spent every possible weekend and evening sailing a Wayfarer which we kept in the harbour. We also sailed with his dad who owned a Westerly Centaur, and were allowed to sail it on our own across the Bristol Channel to Ilfracombe when we were 16! University came and went and then I nipped down to UKSA to get some

qualifications, as although I had sailed over 10,000 miles I had never done any courses. Two days after my RYA Yachtmaster exam, Neilson flew me to Greece, having hired me to work at their resort of Nidri.

What is the day-to-day job of a flotilla skipper?

Flotilla life varies every day and can go from one extreme to the other. The major bonus of working for Neilson as a flotilla skipper is that you are on a two-week rotation. The first week you live ashore in staff accommodation and teach guests on one of our 4-day 'Introduction to Yachting' courses. This is followed by two days off when you can do as you choose. For instance, if you are based in one of our beach resorts you can use all of the kit, go waterskiing, wakeboarding, dinghy sailing and windsurfing, or just chill out, have time to yourself, go exploring or take a yacht away for the night. One perk is that you normally share your room with the skipper on the opposite rotation, so effectively have a room to yourself!

The following week you spend on flotilla, living on the lead boat with your mate and engineer. An 'average day' consists of waking up around 8.30, having a bit of breakfast, catching the weather forecast from the Navtex or office and preparing the whiteboard for our morning flotilla briefing. The briefings are normally around 9.30, although we are happy to adjust if the guests want them earlier or later. Each briefing consists of telling the guests where we are going, how to get there and anything worth seeing on the way. We normally recommend a few places to stop for lunch, and then the guests start to head off on their way.

Once the last guest has gone, we cast off and head to the destination, overtaking them all on the way.

One thing you must be able to do is remain calm at all times and make quick decisions. You are in charge of up to 12 yachts and the lives of up to around 50 guests – it's a big responsibility.

Sometimes it's because we sail better and sometimes it's because there is no wind and we have to motor! We arrive at the destination first and prepare for the guests' arrival. As they come in one by one, we help them moor and provide advice on anything they are unsure about, which normally involves a gin and tonic! The engineer fixes things that might have gone wrong and the mate organises some entertainment. We usually end up in the bar with the guests and have a few beers to celebrate the end of an excellent day.

Would you recommend working on a flotilla as a temporary or full time career?

It is entirely up to you. Some people use flotilla skippering as the first rung in the yachting industry ladder, and then move on to private charter yachts or super yachts. For others it's a gap year job after university, or a career break. Some people, like me, get stuck in the gluepot and work up the ladder in the same company.

What's the money like? Is it a good way to get rich?

As the lifestyle is excellent, you can imagine there are a lot of people around wanting to be a flotilla skipper, which means that the money may not be what you expect. What you have to remember is that Neilson pays for your flights and accommodation as well, so if you include your salary with free rent, water, gas and electricity it's actually quite a lot. All the money you earn is yours to spend on food and drink. You don't need anything else, and on flotilla the restaurants you take guests to will usually provide your meals. Be nice enough to the guests and they will buy you a beer or two as well!

What qualifications are required for the job?

If you are coming into the company from scratch, we generally ask for Yachtmaster or Coastal Skipper, as you will also be providing some yacht instruction. If you don't have any qualifications, then we usually provide an instructor course at the start of the season. You could apply as a mate/host/hostess and progress to skipper the following season, using the first season to learn all the top tips from your skipper.

What experience and personal characteristics are most useful?

I would say flotilla skippering is about 20% sailing knowledge and 80% personality. You need to be outgoing, friendly, and approachable. You will be working with guests all the time, so if you don't like mingling with random people, it may not be for you! It's hard work but great fun. One thing you must be able to do is remain calm at all times and make quick decisions. You

are in charge of up to 12 yachts and the lives of up to around 50 guests – it's a big responsibility. A sudden squall may require you to think on your feet.

What are the best and worst aspects of working on flotilla?

Best things include sunshine (not always!), being outdoors, doing what you love and meeting loads of new people. Worst things include difficult guests and turnaround day, when you have to prepare the yachts for new guests. That's about it really.

Is the flotilla route always the same? Does that get boring?

A major bonus of working for Neilson is that the skipper can choose the route. You can look at weather, where other flotilla companies are sailing, the size of your flotilla and competency of your guests, and then decide your route since we don't have to follow something that's shown in the brochure. It provides variety and helps spread guest money to different harbours.

Do you get friction between the lead boat crew? Surely there is no escape?

We tend to all start working at the same time during 'fit out' – the period when we get the yachts ready for the season. The managers look at how we are interacting and select lead crews based on whoever we get on with best. Because we have a two-week rotation at Neilson, you spend every other week in staff accommodation, so can enjoy time away from your crew if you need to!

Do you get some really stupid, demanding or downright horrible clients?

Sometimes it can be difficult, but remember that for most of the day you are on the lead boat, away from them. You only have to talk to guests in the mornings and evenings, and by about mid week you will usually have done something that impresses them!

It must be difficult managing a flotilla if you get several days of gale force winds. Is that kind of thing a stressful challenge?

Providing you are in a safe harbour, it's no big deal. The mate usually organises activities and if there are some 'die hard dads' you can take a yacht out and get them soaked. That gives the men a lot of stories about "How big the waves were…" to tell at dinner! If bad weather comes out of nowhere, it can catch you out – remain calm and give good, strong advice over the VHF and think about heading to a different harbour to get everybody into shelter more quickly.

What is the typical age for working as flotilla skipper and what are the options for finding other work when you get older?

In my experience, the average age of skippers is mid 20s. At that age you normally would have enough life experience to deal with the guests, guest issues and manage your mate and engineer. That's not to say we don't have people who are a lot older, often on career changes – we had one skipper of 56! Most skippers who move on from flotillas get excellent experience and references and have no trouble finding work on private charter yachts or super yachts. Some move back to the UK to work in the watersports industry, so they can settle down and buy property. But for me – it's too cold and wet!

What advice would you give to someone who would like to work as a flotilla skipper on a gap year or university holiday?

Flotilla skippers have a lot of responsibility and need good management skills, which you may not have acquired if you are on gap year before uni. You could however become a mate, see how you get on and progress to skipper once you have more experience. Neilson also require flotilla skippers to work full season from March through to November, so you can do fit-out (preparing the boats for guests) and lay-up (preparing the boats for the winter). You could also become a yacht instructor for your uni holiday and help cover lead crew holidays.

We usually end up in the bar with the guests and have a few beers to celebrate the end of an excellent day.

Thanks Alex. Any final thoughts or advice?

It's hard work with long hours, but is fun! You meet lots of new people, gain tons of experience and make the best friends. You will have the time of your life, but make sure you think it through and that it's what you want to do. Read lots on Google and find out if anybody at your local sailing club has been a flotilla skipper, so they can tell you all about it. Failing that, you could go to one of the boat shows and talk to skippers who will be on the flotilla company stands.

■ www.neilson.com ❖

FLOTILLA SKIPPER – Sharon Hayward

Skippering a flotilla is no longer an all male preserve! Girls have the opportunity to do a great job as well…

Sharon, can you tell us how you became a skipper on a flotilla?

I worked in marketing for seven years after graduating. From a career perspective, I had a good job working as a manager for well-known brands and was doing well. However, I had a difficult year on a personal level and felt I needed time out – the daily grind of the commute was wearing me down and I wanted some open space. Rather than just go travelling, I decided to do something that would tie in with my new interest in sailing. People told me the Boat Show is a good place to get a job, so I turned up CV in hand and approached a few companies to look for a job as a mate/hostess. I knew I didn't have enough experience to be a skipper, but my aim was to work my way up, which is exactly what happened!

Can you describe your day-to-day work as a flotilla skipper?

The job is seasonal and starts by preparing the boats. This is pretty horrible work, but is a great way to find out how the yachts are put together. When someone has a problem later in the year, you will have a good idea of what could be the issue and how to resolve it. Once the guests arrive, the skipper's role is about ensuring that each flotilla week is a holiday of a lifetime! This covers a range of responsibilities. I have to decide exactly where to go on the flotilla route, taking into account weather forecasts, which may be consulted several times a day if storms are likely. I also have overall responsibility for safety of the guests and boats, so each day starts with a briefing on the route and destination, highlighting both nice lunch stops and hazards along the way. At the end of the day, the skipper has to help guests moor up and ensure their boats are secure for the overnight stay.

It never goes that smoothly. Nearly every day, a guest will call over the VHF with a problem. Sometimes these can be resolved in a matter of minutes. Other problems, like running aground, are a bit more stressful!

Would you recommend working on a flotilla as a temporary or full time career?

Temporary. It's a great way to get into the business and meet like-minded people, and from there you can move into resort management or working on superyachts. Not many people do more than four or five seasons.

Is it a good way to save money?

That depends on your lifestyle. The pay is poor compared to normal jobs, but with accommodation and uniform provided by the company and most food and drink provided by friendly restaurants and generous guests, there isn't much need to spend a lot of money. I managed to live off tips and save my entire salary, leaving me with about £3k after a summer's work, but other people spend their whole salary and more.

What qualifications would you recommend?

I only had Day Skipper when I joined as a mate. You need a First Aid certificate and an instructor qualification would be useful.

What experience and personal characteristics are most useful?

You obviously need sailing experience – the more varied the better. Lots of customer-facing experience is also a real plus. If you aren't used to always being helpful and happy, this kind of work can be surprisingly tiring. You need to relate to people and sense when they are nervous, but too embarrassed to say so. It helps to be confident, but not cocky, with endless energy and enthusiasm. Being able to stay calm under pressure is also really important.

What are the best and worst aspects of working on flotilla?

It's never dull – no two days are ever the same. It's also amazing being active and outside every day with no commuting, no air-conditioned offices and no computer screens. It's sunny and hot as well! Plus, you are working with people who are on holiday and intend to have a great time, so they are happy and friendly and want to socialise. Sitting in a quayside café, watching a spectacular sunset over a beer or two, is hardly the worst job in the world!

The downsides are that you never get much

Neilson

personal space, although the great thing about working for Neilson is that you alternate a week on flotilla with a week of yacht training when you effectively work 9-5 and get regular days off to unwind and relax. Working on flotilla can also be physically draining, especially when it's hot. And it can test your diplomatic skills to their limit if you don't get on with a set of guests.

Do you get friction between the lead boat crew?

Yes, living in such confined quarters can put pressure on interpersonal relationships, but most of the time it's OK. At least with three of you there is always a mediator! I've always got on really well with my crew, but if someone is bugging you it's best to say so and not let tensions escalate – a bit of space and a shared beer resolve most issues.

I'm in my 30s and sharing a boat with two 20-year-old boys may not be my ideal (like running a crèche on top of a flotilla), but you look for the best in everyone and they certainly keep it fun! There are the odd major personality clashes that can negatively impact on the guests' holiday experience, so management are usually as keen to resolve the problems as everyone else. Tolerance and a willingness to adapt your working and living style to ensure harmony certainly helps.

Neilson

Do you get some really stupid, demanding or downright horrible clients?

Oh yes! The most important thing is to maintain professionalism. You never let the guests know you think that about them and absolutely never say anything that could be overheard. This is one of the toughest elements of the job and can require extensive patience and teeth gritting, whilst smiling broadly and laughing along. Sometimes stupidity comes from ignorance, so on many occasions 'stupid' behaviour can be resolved by a spot of training – for example, tips on furling the genoa in strong winds can avoid someone ripping sails or getting whipped in the face by flailing ropes.

It must be difficult managing a flotilla if you get several days of gale force winds?

That's when you really earn your money, but the

guests recognise that you are looking after them and are quite understanding. I had a period of three weeks of storms and I stayed up nearly all night every night, adjusting and checking moorings. The crosswinds were so strong that warps were snapping! You are rarely storm bound for more than one day, so even if you only go a short hop to the next destination at least guests get out on the water. If it's genuinely really rough, the guests often don't want to go out anyway.

What is the ideal age for working as flotilla skipper? What are the options for finding other work when you get older?

At Neilson you have to be 21 or older to be skipper, which is a good thing – being in charge of up to 12 yachts and 60+ people takes a bit of life experience! Ages vary from 23 right up to 65. Those at the younger end of the scale often see this as the starting point in a career, moving on to big boat or superyacht work. Older skippers tend to have different motivations – looking for more of a way of life, after a career in something totally unrelated like myself.

What advice would you give to someone who would like to work as a flotilla skipper on a gap year or university holiday?

I wish I'd done it then! Having engineering skills is a plus. Be prepared to work hard and play hard. Also be prepared to struggle to return to normal life. The more experience you have of being resourceful and working with people the better. Guests love a lead crew with character!

Any final thoughts or advice?

If you've not been on a flotilla, try and go along with a friend on a lead boat for a week to get a real idea of how it is. Then recruiters will know that you understand what you are signing up for.

■ www.neilson.com ❖

YACHT ENGINEER – Matthew Calvert

Matthew works as a lead boat engineer on Sunsail flotillas, with responsibility for keeping everything working smoothly…

Matthew, how did you become an engineer?

I left college at 19 after completing a BTEC national diploma in auto engineering and became an apprentice technician for MG Rover. I was in the garage for just over three years and gained experience working on various different systems on many different vehicles. This was invaluable to the job I am in now.

What is the difference between working as a flotilla and base engineer?

Life as a base engineer is quite different to a flotilla engineer. On base it can be classed as a 9 to 5 job, but in a much better working environment than a flotilla. Once the day's work has finished, there is a large amount of free time to explore the area and have fun, either with water sports or in bars! On base you live in a shared accommodation with other members of staff.

As a base engineer, you may only see

clients when they board their bareboat charter yachts and then return at the end of the holiday. As a flotilla engineer you can be on call 24/7, especially if the weather is bad. For the other 90% of the time, the job really starts when a problem occurs on one of your flotilla yachts or are called out to fix another charter yacht. The jobs vary from squeaky hinges on cupboards to electrical faults and may even include rigging. Frequent service is essential, such as engine and filter checks. As soon as a fault is reported by a customer, it must be seen to have been looked at by the engineer or skipper – sometimes both are required to help. It is very important that problems get fixed as soon as possible to avoid customer dissatisfaction.

What's the money like? Is it a good way to save?

In this job I have found it best not to think about the wages! Yes, the money isn't brilliant and many jobs will pay much more. However, not many jobs offer you work that is excellent experience and an awesome adventure in a fantastic climate. It's worth mentioning that flotilla engineers are not paid as much as skippers, but can be doing as much if not more work. The same goes for the hostess!

If you are a good saver and don't blow your money on booze, fags and other things, then you can make it a well paid job, especially if you are good to the clients! At Sunsail the local pay is just enough to live on, while the rest of your earnings are put into a bank account which you shouldn't need to touch.

> **If you are a good saver and don't blow your money on booze, fags and other things, then you can make it a well paid job…**

What qualifications are required?

Skippers must be fully trained in yacht handling, but engineers only have to pass a small exam during the interview period. I have spoken to engineers who have no qualifications, but most have at least some sort of experience. My opinion is that all engineers should have some form of marine and/or automotive engineering experience, while any safety training such as STCW95 should be offered by the company, since many engineers have never set foot on a boat before. Some engineers are very experienced and offer to 'pass down' their knowledge to those having difficulty.

What experience and personal characteristics are most useful?

Any work on marine or automotive systems is helpful. You must be willing to work hard and want to further your knowledge on marine engineering, as well as being able to socialise with clients and crew.

Personally, the worst jobs are the heads (toilets), but as an engineer you just have to hold your nose and get used to it!

What are the best and worst aspects of working on flotilla?

Personally, I have never looked back since I took this job. The best aspect is relaxing once all the yachts are safely tied up in the afternoon. Once everyone is happy and the yachts are OK, it's time to go eat!

Annoying things are call-outs from other charter yachts. This means having to leave the flotilla to go and fix another yacht, but it's all part of the job. Another drawback is battling with bad weather and storms, but correct procedures help to minimise problems – for instance making sure the yachts are tied up safely. Also, a problem may be reported in the late afternoon and if it's major may take a long time to fix. This means while everyone else is eating, you are stuck fixing the boat. If you have a good crew, they might bring you a takeaway!

It must be tough having your head inside an engine compartment on baking hot days?

Ha! Ha! It's not as bad as you might think. It makes everything worthwhile, because once the job is done you can jump in the sea! You tend to get used to the heat and common problems with yachts. A general knowledge of engines, electrics, plumbing and gas systems are helpful. Personally, the worst jobs are the heads (toilets), but as an engineer you just have to hold your nose and get used to it!

Do you get friction between the lead boat crew on a flotilla?

Yes! And no there isn't much chance of escape. I have had quite a few different hostesses and skippers, but always tried to get along with all of them.

Whatever happens don't take sides with one person! A good relationship with your crew is very important. Both the skipper, engineer and hostess work together to get the job done and keep people happy. If the crew are not happy, clients will notice and may report this at the end of their holiday.

Do you change roles or just stick with working as the engineer?

I have only worked as the engineer, though my last hostess tried to teach me how to cook and in return I taught her about basic systems on the yachts. Most of the time, the skipper and engineer take it in turn to helm and moor the boat – normally the one who does not have a

It is very important that problems get fixed as soon as possible to avoid customer dissatisfaction.

hangover! Role changes can occur if one crew member falls ill, so it would be an advantage if training is given to the engineer and hostess to Day Skipper level.

Do you get clients who do things like running out of diesel or blocking the heads? Is that annoying?

It happens all the time. No matter how much you brief clients on the do's and dont's, things like this always happen. It's why the flotilla engineer is there! A common problem is people accidentally turning on the autopilot and wondering why they cannot turn the yacht.

Do you ever get major problems with a boat, which means it cannot continue with a flotilla?

It is rare but does happen. Sometimes it's accidental damage from the client; on rarer occasions it's failure of a major system on the yacht.

How does being a flotilla or base engineer compare with working as an engineer on a crewed yacht?

I have never worked on a crewed yacht, but I can imagine that being a flotilla engineer is much more relaxed as it's seasonal work. The lead boat becomes your home for the season and you make it your own. On a crewed yacht, that isn't really possible.

What are the options for finding other work when you want to progress your career?

Ultimately, it depends on what you want to go into as a full time career. As an engineer there is always work available. For a short term 'gap year' job working as a flotilla or base engineer is great, but a little harder if you want to make it into a full time career. More consideration needs to be given to pay and what to do during the winter season. Personally, I've always been willing to go on any courses that will progress my career.

What advice would you give to someone who would like to work as an engineer?

Work as a base or flotilla engineer is awesome. My advice would be to try it out. You must have some basic engineering experience and be willing to work long and sometimes difficult hours. It is possible for gap year students to work at this job for a great experience, but don't confuse it with a holiday! Remember that all three lead crew are responsible for the yachts and the clients.

In doing this job, you get to meet some fantastic people and have an amazing experience. If you want to work and travel all over the world, then this job is ideal. Yes, at times people do get homesick, especially when times are hard. Battle through and you will not regret it.

■ www.sunsail.com ❖

HOSTESS – Amy Packard

The hostess or mate manages the social programme of the flotilla, including parties and barbecues, looks after the clients' welfare and helps with travel or domestic problems. Amy Packard sees this job from both sides of the fence, working as a Sunsail Flotilla Hostess in summer and Sunsail Recruitment Advisor in winter…

Amy, can you tell us how you became a hostess on a flotilla?

After my A levels, I went to work for Barclays Bank for three years. I started in their administration department, working up to coordinating all the in-house training courses for Barclays Wealth Management in the Isle of Man. When I was unfortunately made redundant from Barclays, I applied for a flotilla hostess role.

Having grown up in a sailing family and seen the job in action during a few holidays with Sunsail, I decided it would allow me to combine my love of sailing with my knowledge of customer service.

What does working as a flotilla hostess entail?

A lot of organisational and communication skills and patience are a must. Preparing twelve yachts for your next flotilla, meeting and greeting clients on transfer days, briefings, organising group meals, punch parties, onshore activities for the kids and adults (as they all turn into big kids on holiday) in the evenings, BBQs and catering for up to 70 guests on a 35 foot lead boat can be a challenge, but is great fun. Plus dealing with complaints when they arise, helping moor up yachts in the evenings with your skipper and always doing a lot of smiling, talking and socialising with clients.

Would you recommend working a flotilla hostess?

Of course I would. If you are looking for a great adventure for the summer working overseas in Greece, Turkey, Croatia or the Caribbean for a season, then look into it. It's definitely not for the little hearted – there is a lot of hard work and you are not on a holiday! You have big responsibility and have to work long hours, looking after your clients and ensuring they have a fantastic time.

What's the money like?

The money is not great. If you are worried about not earning much, stop and ask yourself if it's the right job before going any further.

It's definitely not for the little hearted – there is a lot of hard work! You have big responsibility and have to work long hours…

A Sunsail flotilla leaves harbour in Croatia. The lead boat crew must always be first in and last out, making sure their clients are always looked after and entertained.

But once on flotilla your outgoings are very small and Sunsail look after you very well, as do all of the locals on your flotilla route. They treat you like one of their own for six months – the number of surrogate fathers (restaurant owners) I had is quite funny. Your flights, accommodation, uniform and insurance are all included in the package, so you just have to cover food and drink.

Some of your wages are paid locally each week, which will see you through the season nicely, while the remainder is paid monthly back in the UK. During three seasons I never dipped into my bank account at home. Most recently, I even managed to pay rent on my house in the UK and work overseas – just!

What qualifications, experience and characteristics are most useful?

Qualifications on the hostess side are none. However coming into this job with sailing skills is very useful. Competent Crew level is all you really need, just so you know that you will be happy to live and work on a yacht and are still going to enjoy it when the weather becomes the opposite of flat calm with sparkly blue seas. You also have to be a very sociable and chatty person with great organisational skills, and be willing to sort out problems that may arise away from base, either by yourself or within your team of three. Thinking quickly on your feet is required all of the time.

Sunsail

only dream of doing. It's not great when a client has a problem, either with their yacht or holiday, but as with all jobs you take the rough with the smooth and deal with the situation to the best of your ability.

Do you get friction between the lead boat crew?

Yes you can! But if you go into your season with an open mind and don't get wound up by small things, then you'll be fine. If things get tense, then talk about it face to face when you have all calmed down. In the last few seasons we made a little chill-out zone on the yacht. If any one of us sat forward of the mast, we were up there for our own time and not to be disturbed – it worked a treat.

What are the best and worst aspects of working on flotilla?

Best is hard to put into a sentence. Just being part of someone's holiday and making it special is great, and by doing the smallest things to help. For instance, taking the children off to do a model boat competition whilst their parents sit with their gin and tonics, watching the sun set in a small harbour in Greece, is amazing. Socialising and getting to know your clients is good as well – you get to meet and see some fantastic people and places.

Worst is not having a day off in six months. Even though you have time away from your clients during the day and on free sailing days, it's quite difficult to get away from it all and this can get you down. However, just have a quiet word with yourself and remember where you are and the opportunity you have been given to experience, which is something many people

Do you get some really stupid, demanding or downright horrible clients?

I wouldn't call them stupid, but they can be very inexperienced. Occasional clients slip through the sales team and bluff about their sailing experience, claiming they are better than they really are. But that's why you are there – to help them, when they realise they can't steer their yacht in reverse in a straight line, don't know how to hoist the sails or tie a mooring line to a cleat. You just have to remain very calm and see the funny side of it. I used to run mini master classes on how to tie bowlines, while my skipper ran mooring stern-to practice classes for those who wished to learn. That not only makes them feel better, but also makes your life easier in the evenings. Some clients seem to have endless problems, ranging from things that are genuinely our fault to things that appear to be completely hyped up. These people may be demanding, but it's their holiday and they want it to be great and run smoothly, which is what you are there for. Forward thinking can avoid a huge amount of such problems.

Some clients seem to have endless problems, ranging from things that are genuinely our fault to things that appear to be completely hyped up…

How does being a flotilla hostess compare with working as a hostess on a crewed yacht?

I see flotilla as being much more fun, because it's interactive with your clients, hands-on and you get a little more freedom throughout the days. Crewed yachts are at a much higher level of customer service. You have to be very well presented, cleaning, cooking and tidying at all times, with very limited freedom. But you only work for one set of clients during a week's charter, instead of looking after sixty clients living on a fleet of twelve yachts!

What advice would you give to someone who would like to work as a flotilla hostess?

The Mediterranean season runs from April through to November and you need to be available for a full summer. The role is very competitive. You would need to show good customer service experience in previous roles, good product knowledge, great communication skills and maturity at interview. Always remember

You would need to show good customer service experience in previous roles, good product knowledge, great communication skills and maturity at interview.

that clients can be very demanding and you are left to think on your own feet a lot of the time. You must also be happy about working away from home for six months and forget the hair straighteners, lip-gloss and home comforts!

I would almost suggest looking at a season in one of our Sunsail clubs, first as an activities assistant or kids' club assistant. That way you can get to see our products running side by side, experience the type of clients and learn how to deal with day-to-day queries and complaints.

Do you have any tips on choosing between jobs with different flotilla operators?

Look into where the companies are based worldwide, the type and number of yachts they have and how long they have been running. Check what the company can offer in terms of benefits and ongoing seasonal work, such as winter or full time opportunities.

What is the typical age for working as a flotilla hostess? What are the options for finding other work when you get older?

Typical age is 20 to 35 years old. It is certainly suited for younger people, but if you are slightly older, young at heart and fancy a career change, there is nothing stopping you. If you are looking for that next challenge, it may be time to progress to working on crewed yachts with a partner.

Working on flotilla in the summer and working in the Sunsail office in the winter sounds a neat combination. Would you recommend going in that direction?

The UK office only has a few vacancies over the winter and they are mainly with sales teams, so I was very lucky that a position in recruitment came up after my second season. However, working for Sunsail over the summer and doing a ski season over the winter would be a fantastic combination. As Sunsail is now part of the ever-growing TUI Travel PLC, then the opportunities are endless with almost 200 companies to choose from!

■ www.tuitraveljobs.com ❖

Surf www.rya.org.uk for information on how to get Competent Crew, Day Skipper, Coastal Skipper and Yachtmaster qualifications.

RYA

YACHT DELIVERY

Delivery skippers usually operate on a freelance basis, but some delivery companies are large enough to employ staff. Qualifications required by the skipper will vary depending on the distance involved, but the RYA Yachtmaster Offshore certificate of competence with commercial endorsement should be regarded as the minimum requirement. Delivery skippers often require additional crew, which can provide a great opportunity to build experience. It may help to have a trade such as electrician, boat builder or engineer.

DELIVERING BOATS FOR A LIVING
Paul Merritt

It's a great way to work in fine weather…

Paul Merritt has been delivering sail and motor yachts for four decades. This is his guide to a tricky and challenging profession.

Getting started…

It was around 1969 when I delivered my first boat, a small 20-foot gaffer, from Cowes to Poole. In those days you didn't need any qualifications. I had lived on a houseboat on the River Itchen in Southampton and been involved with the Sea Scouts for some time, doing all my learning from books such as Nicholls Seamanship, Reeds Nautical Almanac and whatever I could lay my hands on, while picking up experience by crewing and skippered yachts at Cowes.

Since those early days I now hold certificates for RYA Powerboat level 2, Yachtmaster

Commercial, Boatmaster for full UK waters and most recently an STCW95 officer of the watch for 3000 tons unlimited. In terms of experience, I must have covered in excess of 500,000 nautical miles while working in many different fields. I drive tugs, dredgers, pilot boats and fishing vessels. I do sea trials on new vessels for Azimut, Fairline and other companies. I also do hand-overs on new boats, which may be delivered with the owner or my own crew.

Ocean Delivery

My company Ocean Delivery was set up in 1999. I had been living and working in France, when I came back and decided it was time to be my own boss again. I knew lots of people and found work easy to get delivering Hallberg-Rasseys, Maxis and lots more. My big break came in 2001 when Peters, a major yacht agency, phoned to ask if I was available to do a demo. I was taken out for a test drive to see if I was up to scratch! Since that day I have not stopped working and was introduced to the big boys. I also met all the editors from yachting mags and now do occasional articles for them.

Ocean Delivery undertakes all sorts of work. When the credit crunch hit in 2008, deliveries and handovers became more rare so I started driving tugs for Williams Shipping in Southampton, dredgers for M.L. Dredging and the occasional pilot boat. My main purpose is still yacht delivery and I have done two really good ones in the past year – taking an Azimut 85 from Portsmouth to Gibraltar and a Fairline Squadron 68 from Jersey to Barcelona – plus lots of smaller deliveries around the coast and across the Channel. To round off the year, I also look after a few boats during the winter lay-up and organise work to be done on them.

As a career
I get e-mails all the time from people seeking work and wanting to come along as crew to get miles for their Yachtmaster. They all seem to think that once you get that certificate, work will flood in. It doesn't! It has taken me nearly forty years to earn a reasonable living and I still have to combine it with other work. But as a career, I couldn't think of anything better, once you are established.

Best and Worst
Best is undoubtedly cruising at twenty knots across the Bay of Biscay or down the Portuguese coast in a brand new boat with blue skies, warm air and flat seas, heading for a port in southern Spain or Italy. Worst is crossing the North Sea with a dodgy forecast in an old dog of a boat, when it's freezing cold and you're trying to get a meal together. The other worst time is

It has taken me nearly forty years to earn a reasonable living and I still have to combine it with other work. But as a career, I couldn't think of anything better, once you are established.

when you're in a foreign port, trying to sort out engine problems, watching the good weather passing by, with the owner on the phone wanting to know how things are progressing.

Sail or Power?
Nowadays I prefer power. The pay is better and you are normally in port every night. I still do the occasional yacht delivery, but pick and choose what kind of yacht and delivery to take on.

Opportunities
A few years ago, there were opportunities to get a foot in the door, but it then became extremely hard with the economic downturn. To get started, you must be prepared to do things cheaply and of course take on almost anything – as long as it's seaworthy! You can expect to get paid. Nobody does anything for nothing, but do not expect good rates until you are well established.

Overnight stop and the accommodation doesn't look bad!

Problems

Not so much nowadays, but I had plenty of problems when I first started. I would deliver almost anything that floated and consequently suffered engine breakdowns, ripping sails and broken rigging. I did walk off one 60-foot motorboat a couple of years ago. Having picked it up in Barcelona for delivery to Southampton, there were oil leaks, water coming in through the stern glands and fuel tanks leaking into the bilges after the first day on passage to Denia. You have to be hard in these situations and say, "I am ending this job here!" The owner was with me and was not too pleased, but it is your reputation that is at stake.

Timetable

You must try to get the boat delivered in the time scale quoted, but I will not put to sea with a bad forecast. You also have to remember that when the owner last saw his boat in the UK, it was probably new and in pristine condition.

You must be prepared to start at the bottom. Wash dishes or whatever it takes to get a position on a good delivery of over a thousand miles.

He expects the same when it arrives at the destination! He does not want doors hanging off or broken galley appliances, because you decided to put to sea with a Force 8 forecast. However, sometimes you will get caught out – it's inevitable.

Ending up in gaol

You do hear of this happening to delivery crews. It has never happened to me, but I am getting more and more cautious. I will not leave with any locked cupboards because "The owner has his personal effects in them…" and demand keys for everything. If I pick up a strange boat I

will also check everything. I insist all paperwork is correct – registration documents, insurance documents, letter of authority, all lifesaving equipment in date and working, VAT paperwork and everything else.

We are getting asked for more and more paperwork, especially in France and Portugal. Recently, for the first time ever, I was asked to produce my Yachtmaster certificate!

Advice

n If I was just starting now, I would straight away sign up for a week at Warsash Maritime Centre or somewhere similar and do the STCW 95 sea survival, first aid, firefighting and personal/social responsibility courses. Everyone is asking for these qualifications now and I won't employ any crew without sea survival and first aid.

n You must be prepared to start at the bottom. Wash dishes or whatever it takes to get a position on a good delivery of over a thousand miles. Once you have done this first big delivery, things will get easier.

n Look, learn and listen. Keep a log and get references from skippers along the way. Get a few deliveries under your belt and then do your Yachtmaster. There are so many people walking around with Yachtmaster certificates who have no experience at all – you can't do a week's course in the Solent and expect to be competent!

Watch out

Beware of deliveries where daddy has a boat and his son or daughter is on holiday from university and willing to do a delivery job for food and flights home. These are getting fewer and fewer, as insurance companies are clamping down heavily. Above all else, make certain that the skipper is insured to deliver the boat and has this in writing with his or her name on the certificate.

Above all else, make certain that the skipper is insured to deliver the boat and has this in writing with his or her name on the certificate.

Best job

My best delivery ever was without doubt a Fairline Squadron 55 from Hamble to Lanzarote. Brilliant weather all the way calling at Lorient, Gijon, Bayona, Cascais, Vilamoura, Gibraltar, Mohamadia (Morocco), Agadir (Morocco) and Lanzarote. We even stopped one hundred and fifty miles out in the Bay of Biscay and had a barbeque. Whales, dolphins and flying fish for company, ending with two days in the owner's apartment with swimming pool in Lanzarote, before flying home.

Worst job

Bringing the same boat back! Bad weather all the way. Got caught in the tail end of a hurricane crossing to Morocco, even though the forecast was good. Lost the radar, GPS and autopilot and had seawater coming through the internal lights in the saloon. On arrival in Morocco we had problems getting fuel and even worse moored too close to the king's boat and were nearly arrested. I was never more pleased than arriving in Gibraltar and mainland Europe.

Joining a delivery
- Check who the skipper is.
- Do they have insurance?
- How long have they been delivering boats?
- What is their experience?
- Does the boat have all the necessary safety equipment?
- What is the duration of the voyage and what time of year?

- www.oceandelivery.co.uk ❖

"Watch out, that's an albatross."
A yacht instructor has to be
prepared…

RYA

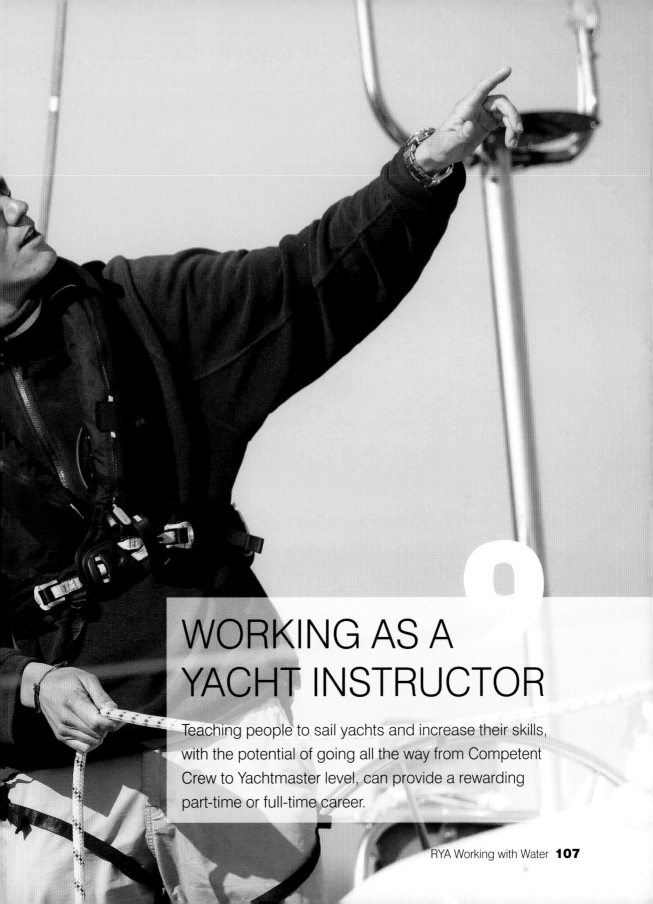

WORKING AS A
YACHT INSTRUCTOR

Teaching people to sail yachts and increase their skills, with the potential of going all the way from Competent Crew to Yachtmaster level, can provide a rewarding part-time or full-time career.

RYA CHIEF CRUISING INSTRUCTOR
Simon Jinks

Simon, how did you get to your current position?

I started sailing dinghies as a lad in Birmingham. I was pretty disillusioned with working in a factory so decided to work for a tenth of the pay and teach dinghy sailing. That was over twenty years ago and since then I've worked in most parts of the marine industry, running yachts overseas, deliveries, lots of teaching and managing schools. I qualified to teach on yachts and motorboats around 1990 and became an examiner in 1999. During the last ten years I have had the pleasure of going afloat with some of the best skippers in the world, whilst running instructor courses. I write books and also articles for Yachting Monthly where I was Technical Writer, as well as other power and sail magazines. I started full time with the RYA in 2004.

What does your job at the RYA involve?

I manage the practical and shore based Yachtmaster Cruising scheme for leisure and commercial use up to 24 metres. About 70,000 courses are run all over the world each year and it takes around 5,000 instructors at 1,500 RYA recognised schools to supply this demand. To ensure the standards of training are maintained, a team of 12 inspectors annually inspects all those schools teaching practical courses. Another team of trainers instructs and updates instructors. My day job is working with a great staff of dedicated people to make sure this all happens.

What kind of temperament is required to work as an instructor in the Cruising scheme?

You need integrity. You also need to be fair, honest, dedicated and have a good sense of humour.

Do you get situations where cruising instructors fail to match the required standards and may risk losing their qualification?

All instructors have to pass their instructor training to get started. Occasionally, some may break our code of conduct and face a disciplinary panel.

What kind of job opportunities are available for people who want to work as instructors?

There are opportunities to teach on a part-time basis or make it a full-time career in the UK or overseas. Many instructors go on to become examiners or run large vessels. Yachtmaster Instructors can be very sought after individuals.

What advice would you give to someone who is interested in working as a cruising instructor?

Experience is key. Get as much experience as possible and then go for a certificate of competence with a commercial endorsement. Once you have some time under your belt from skippering commercially, consider enrolling on a Cruising Instructor course. ❖

About 70,000 courses are run all over the world each year and it takes around 5,000 instructors at 1,500 RYA recognised schools to supply this demand.

QUALIFYING AS AN RYA CRUISING AND YACHTMASTER INSTRUCTOR

Cruising Instructor

Minimum Age: 18

■ **Essential requirements:** First aid certificate; Yachtmaster® Offshore certificate of competence; commercial endorsement; basic sea survival certificate; medical fitness examination; maximum age limit of 64.

■ **Useful qualifications:** RYA diesel and radar certificates.

Sail Cruising instructors are able to teach the Start Yachting, Competent Crew and Day Skipper practical courses at an RYA recognised training centre. The liveaboard course takes five days. Motor Cruising instructors are able to teach the Helmsman's and Day Skipper power courses at an RYA recognised training centre. The course takes two days. Both qualifications are valid for five years.

Yachtmaster® Instructor

Minimum Age: 18

■ **Essential requirements:** First aid certificate; Yachtmaster® Offshore certificate of competence; commercial endorsement; basic sea survival certificate; medical fitness examination; Cruising Instructor certificate; more than 7,000 miles experience; maximum age limit of 64.

■ **Useful qualifications:** RYA diesel and radar certificates.

Yachtmaster® instructors are able to teach all practical RYA Cruising Scheme courses at RYA recognised training centres, with separate endoresments for sail and motor cruisers. Courses are normally five days for sail and three days for power. The retirement age for Yachtmaster® Instructors is 70.

COMMERCIAL ENDORSEMENT

A commercial endorsement on your RYA certificate of competence enables you to work on commercial vessels. On British flagged vessels operating in the UK or in many non-UK ports, an RYA certificate of competence with a standard commercial endorsement fulfils all legal requirements.

Which certificates can be commercially endorsed?
■ RYA Yachtmaster® Ocean certificate of competence.
■ RYA Yachtmaster® Offshore certificate of competence.
■ RYA Yachtmaster® Skipper certificate of competence.
■ RYA Day Skipper (tidal) practical course completion certificate.
■ RYA Day Skipper (non-tidal) practical course completion certificate, supported by a Day Skipper shorebased course completion certificate.
■ RYA Advanced Powerboat certificate of competence.
■ RYA Powerboat Level 2 course completion certificate.
■ RYA Yachtmaster® Offshore and Yachtmaster® Ocean certificates can receive the STCW endorsement.

Application for standard commercial endorsement

Send the following items to RYA Certification, RYA House, Ensign Way, Hamble, Hampshire SO31 4YA:

■ Original certificate to be commercially endorsed.
■ Commercial endorsement application form.
■ Basic Sea Survival certificate.
■ ML5 or ENG1 medical fitness certificate.
■ Passport sized photo with your name on the back.
■ Fee as shown on application form.

STCW endorsement

Some marine administrations require STCW (Standards of Training, Certification and Watchkeeping for Seafarers 1995) qualifications. Holders of commercially endorsed RYA Yachtmaster® Offshore and Yachtmaster® Ocean certificates of competence can obtain an additional endorsement to comply with STCW95 if they hold the following certificates:

■ STCW personal safety and social responsibilities (half day course).
■ STCW elementary first aid (one day course).
■ STCW fire fighting and fire prevention (2 day course).

HAMBLE SCHOOL OF YACHTING
Rob Gaffney

Rob, how did you get involved with yacht training and instruction?

It's a long story and more by accident than design! I had sailed since a youngster, first in dinghies then cruising and racing yachts. I continued my sailing in the Royal Navy and upon leaving the RN got a mundane job in retail logistics, followed by a series of other varied and at times interesting jobs. However, it became apparent that I wanted a bit more from life, so I decided to leave my job to spend a year doing something I really enjoyed… sailing.

I attended a local sailing school in order to get my Yachtmaster qualification with a view to getting a berth on a yacht headed somewhere nice, then set off across the Atlantic as crew on a small yacht. Later, I returned to the UK and got in touch with the same sailing school to get advice on what I could do with my qualification and experience to try and earn some money. The principal had a long chat and finally advised that I would make a good instructor, so I completed an on-water assessment and passed. Just one week later I was taking my first crew of trainees for a week's sail training. I was a lot more nervous than they were, but must have

hidden it well because the school asked me back again and again.

Over the next few years I split my time between teaching and delivering yachts all over the world. Out of the blue, one of the schools I had worked for asked me to be their chief instructor. Since then I have been involved full time with training and the RYA scheme and am now co-owner of my school.

What services does Hamble School of Yachting provide?

The school offers the full range of RYA training courses for sail cruising, powerboat and motor cruising. We also run MCA/STCW courses as well as a wide range of specialist courses such as offshore safety training, sail trim, boat handling and so on.

Is running a school of yachting a good business? What are the best and worst aspects of your job? Is it closer to 9-5 or 24/7?

Running a school is an immensely satisfying career. Whilst you are very unlikely to ever become rich, the reward is seeing literally hundreds of people develop their skills and confidence whilst taking courses. It's great to see very nervous people on the first evening return after five days with huge smiles on their faces! On the downside, running a school is definitely not 9-5 and you have to be prepared to put in a huge number of hours on any day of the week at any time of the day or night. With up to 13 yachts out at any one time there is always something going on that demands my attention. As with any business, there is also a huge amount of paperwork and administration, so I guess one of the downsides is that despite owning a sailing school I often don't get time to get out and sail!

Running a school is an immensely satisfying career. Whilst you are very unlikely to ever become rich, the reward is seeing literally hundreds of people develop their skills and confidence...

What kind of jobs are available for people who want to work with Hamble School of Yachting?

We employ a core of full and part time support staff who work behind the scenes to keep the school running smoothly. These jobs include accounts, course advisors, catering and of course a team who look after and maintain the yachts which is a huge task in itself. We also employ a chief instructor and several other instructors who teach either on board yachts or in the classroom.

During the busy summer season we expand the number of instructors massively as business builds. All of these temporary instructors are well known to us and have in many cases been trained at the school. For people with the correct teaching qualifications, the summer can be a useful chance to earn money whilst on a gap year or between jobs. We also take on an apprentice during the summer months to work with the maintenance staff in preparing and fixing boats during this busy time. This is a great way for somebody to get involved with the industry and possibly take things further.

What kind of skills and temperament are required to work as a yacht instructor? What qualifications are vital or desirable?

To work as a Yacht Instructor teaching the first three levels of the RYA scheme up to Day Skipper, you are required to hold a commercially endorsed Yachtmaster Offshore Certificate of Competence with a Cruising Instructor endorsement. The Cruising Instructor qualification is carried out by many RYA Training Centres and is run over anything up to 5 or 6 days, and whilst being primarily an assessment is also designed to teach you how to instruct RYA courses. To teach beyond Day Skipper, you will need to upgrade to the RYA Yachtmaster

Getting into the industry can seem quite tough at first and is very much reliant on word of mouth and proving yourself.

Instructor qualification, which can normally be done after several seasons of teaching with the Cruising Instructor qualification. This qualification will also enable you to teach both the Day Skipper and Coastal Skipper/Yachtmaster shore based courses.

Aside from the mandatory qualifications, perhaps the most important thing to possess is the desire to teach and get on with people. On an RYA cruising course, you will be living in very close quarters with total strangers for long periods of time and this brings its own demands. In addition, you will be working long hours in often adverse conditions with students of varying abilities and aptitudes. An instructor must possess endless patience and good humour! The ability to put people at ease, always appear calm and communicate in a clear and concise way is absolutely vital if you are to be a successful instructor.

What advice would you give to a young person who is coming up to leaving school and wants to work with a yachting school?

I would suggest that they develop their skills by sailing dinghies through a local sailing club. This can also give the opportunity to crew aboard yachts, as boat owners are always after extra crew for racing or just cruising. It is a good idea to get involved with the Sea Cadets or possibly a sail training group belonging to ASTO (Association of Sea Training Organisations). These guys often run larger boats that specialise in sail training for youngsters from disadvantaged backgrounds or the disabled. Working aboard one of their boats gives the opportunity to gain funding to get the training needed to rise up the ranks. They run a great scheme known as the Skippership Scheme that aims to develop tomorrow's skippers.

The earliest age at which you can sit the Yachtmaster exam is 18. Having a couple of years of varied and interesting sailing behind you will really help your chances of getting employment at a school or charter company.

Any advice you would like to add?

You need to remain committed. Getting into the industry can seem quite tough at first and is very much reliant on word of mouth and proving yourself. Never turn down an opportunity that will expand your experience and CV. Many of these opportunities are on a voluntary basis, so if you are young the support of parents will be vital. Always do the job in hand to the very best of your ability, even if it is cleaning out the bilges in the bottom of the boat. Work hard, have a positive attitude and you will get noticed. Once you are noticed, word gets around quickly and opportunities will soon start to appear. Never give up!

■ www.hamble.co.uk   ❖

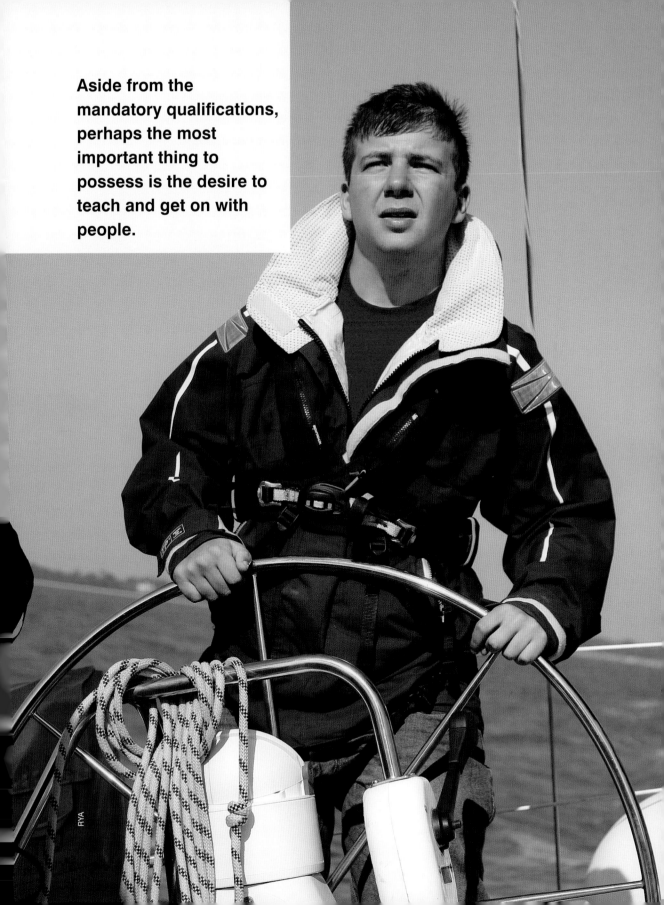

Aside from the mandatory qualifications, perhaps the most important thing to possess is the desire to teach and get on with people.

Time to relax. Geoff Hales takes time off from working on water on board his small yacht Vasco, named after the ship that saved his life…

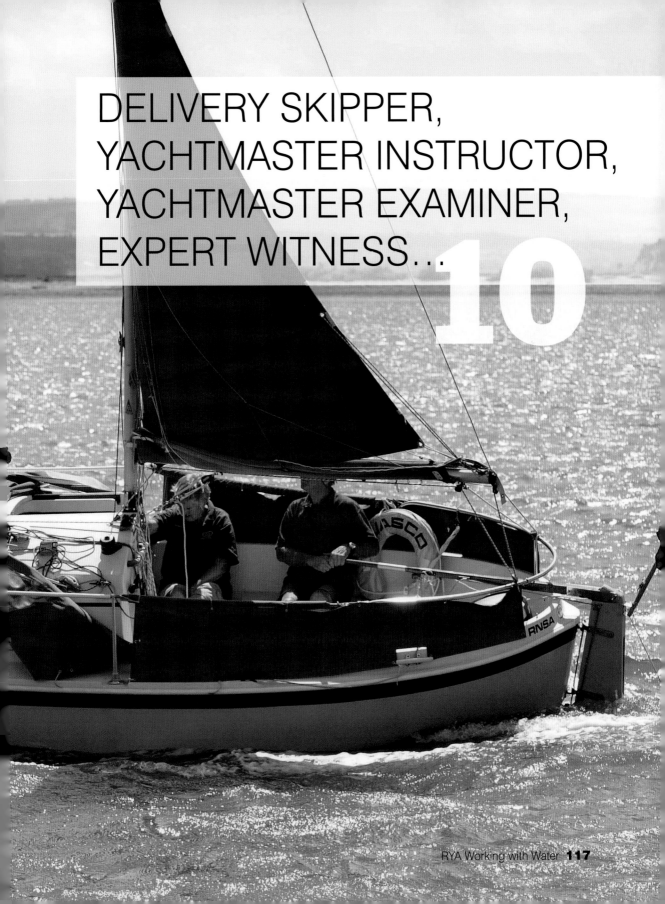

DELIVERY SKIPPER, YACHTMASTER INSTRUCTOR, YACHTMASTER EXAMINER, EXPERT WITNESS…

10

ONE THING CAN LEAD TO ANOTHER

Geoff Hales has enjoyed a varied and action packed sailing career, which started when he developed a liking for long passages as a teenager.

In 1975 Geoff was given leave by the Royal Navy to race a borrowed Nicholson 36 single-handed in the first AZAB (Azores and back race). Having met Rival designer Peter Brett in the Azores, Geoff then raced his 4 year old prototype deep draught Rival 34 in the 1976 OSTAR single-handed transatlantic race, which was the roughest on record, with two competitors lost. He finished 23rd out of 126 starters, but only 73 finishers, and won the handicap prize. He was awarded an MBE and decided it was time to leave the navy and concentrate on professional sailing.

Geoff became sales manager for Rival Yachts, which allowed him to race a Rival 38 in the 1978 2-handed Round Britain Race, followed by the 1979 AZAB single-handed when he finished under jury rig but was not last home. In 1980 Geoff switched jobs and became Yachting World's Technical Editor.

Geoff had always been lucky enough to borrow boats, but eventually decided to go for broke with a second mortgage by commissioning and partly self-building his own short-handed racing machine, choosing a 30-foot water-ballasted hull with a monstrous rig. At the same time he was making a living by writing about boats and teaching novices how to handle their own yachts or powercraft. A grateful client stepped in to sponsor Geoff's new lightweight flyer as Minitech, which had a shake-down in the 1988 Round Britain Race. This was followed by the 1989 2-handed Transat, when Minitech led its class until the forestay broke.

Two years later Geoff entered Minitech for the AZAB. He also had a new job as a part time magazine editor and agreed to race 2-handed with his publisher Andrew Webster. It was a tough call. Minitech's keel fell off close to the Azores, forcing the two crewmen to jump into Geoff's seven year old Tinker Tramp inflatable tender. Their EPIRB filled up with water within an hour, leaving Geoff and Andrew with no way to summon help. They survived because Andrew managed to recover three little bottles of beer, a can of lychees and a bottle of French dressing. After six days they were spotted by a Portuguese military plane and rescued by the warship 'Vasco de Gama'. Since then, all Geoff's boats have been named 'Vasco'.

Geoff has kept busy working as a yachting writer, delivery skipper, instructor and examiner in yachts and powerboats. In addition, he works as an expert witness for boat accidents. The only downside of having so much work is that it leaves very little time to enjoy sailing.

Zero to hero

Having worked as a Yachtmaster Instructor since 1977 and Examiner since 1986, like many others Geoff is not impressed by the 'zero to hero' concept of paying a large amount of money to be crammed with knowledge and hope to earn a Yachtmaster certificate in a few months. He believes that experience should be built up over a long period of time, in a variety of boats and sailing areas, and recommends getting the Coastal Skipper Practical certificate long before undertaking Yachtmaster Offshore. (The Coastal Skipper qualification is sufficient to start working for a large yacht operator such as Sunsail or Neilson, with commercial endorsement requiring sea survival and medical certificates.)

One good reason for signing on for zero to hero courses is that they provide the yachts and passage making necessary to qualify as a Yachtmaster.

Geoff's work as a Yachtmaster Instructor and Examiner provides frequent trips to the Mediterranean. On this occasion he takes the wheel of an Austrian yacht.

As an alternative, Geoff suggests building up experience as a delivery crew after the Coastal Skipper exam. The most you can expect is to have expenses covered, but you have the opportunity to log hundreds of miles on different kinds of yachts for free and learn about 'quick fix' running repairs, compatability and tolerance. These are basics which may demonstrate that you don't want a career afloat after all!

Yacht delivery

Geoff likes to do one 'interesting' delivery every year to learn about new gear and electronics. This kind of work is invariably word of mouth and Geoff is always extremely careful to ensure the boat will be safe enough for the crew to make the delivery. There must also be no danger of being involved with drugs. If there is any doubt, Geoff advises making an extremely thorough check of the boat before commencing a delivery, ideally with the aid of a customs sniffer dog. If the worst happens and you discover drugs on board during a delivery, there may be three unappetising options. Go back, tell the customs and hope they believe the story; throw the drugs over the side and continue, with possible gangster retribution on arrival; continue, pretend you have never found the drugs and hope the customs don't come on board. We all know of crews who have been caught, innocent or otherwise, and spent months or years languishing in foreign gaols.

If Geoff decides a boat is unseaworthy, of course he will refuse to start the delivery until the problems are sorted. In this respect he advises that flying out to join a boat you have never seen and joining a skipper or owner you have never met is likely to be dodgy. Remember, that your life is at risk and many deliveries are not easy at all.

If he is dissatisfied, Geoff will decline the job and recommend transporting the yacht by truck instead. Given the choice, unlike most delivery skippers, Geoff prefers to sail as 'advisor' to the owner who can help sort out problems peculiar to his boat and will know why it stayed in harbour longer than planned. However, the relationship may become tricky if the owner wants to overrule the delivery skipper on how to sail the boat.

Geoff charges a daily rate and does not work for delivery companies which only pay a flat fee for the whole job. He believes this puts the crew under pressure to deliver the boat as quickly and as cheaply as possible, and cautions that some delivery companies do not provide much in the way of safety equipment. Geoff warns that delivery to a very tight budget can also make delivering a powercraft particularly disagreeable. The skipper has to run the engine at optimum revs for minimum fuel consumption, which means the boat can only motor at a slow pace. This is not only boring, but creates a very unpleasant motion as the boat rolls on every wave. The moral is that it's generally more pleasant to deliver a sailing yacht.

Yachtmaster Instructor

Geoff has "enormous admiration" for instructors who have to attempt to get four or five people up to the required level, while preparing for their chosen exam. The instructor has full responsibility for crew and yacht throughout a five day course and is effectively on 24-hour call. In Geoff's view the economics of running a sailing school are very difficult. He takes his hat off to flotilla skippers who also have a very tough job with enormous responsibility. But if you like the idea of working as a Yachtmaster Instructor and don't mind low pay, Geoff

reckons job satisfaction can be very good.

As a well established instructor with strong recommendations, Geoff mostly specialises in helping owners to become confident with their new yachts or powerboats. This may range from a weekend manoeuvring in marinas and picking up buoys, to four or five days working through every aspect of boat handling.

One thing every instructor needs to be careful about is insurance cover, particularly when you are doing 'own boat' teaching. Accidents happen and as Geoff says it's important to be clear about, "Who pays if you ding the boat?" To ensure there will be no disagreement, the instructor must be insured as 'alternative skipper'. And when the instruction is complete, there are two moments of intense relief. First, when you realise there are no more opportunities for bashing the boat, and second when you collect the fee!

One of the obvious downsides of working as a Yachtmaster Examiner is having to fail candidates…

Yachtmaster Examiner

Geoff qualified as a Yachtmaster Examiner in 1986. As with any qualification, true ability will be variable and he strongly approves of examiners being reassessed every five years.

An examiner is paid a flat fee by the RYA for each candidate. In return, the examiner spends anything from 24 to 48 hours on board a yacht assessing the candidates.

As with instruction, Geoff says it's important to be clear about insurance cover and personal responsibility. Repeated attempts at manoeuvres makes a yacht vulnerable to damage. Geoff also favours an intensive 24 hours of assessment, without letting his candidates off the boat, always spending a few hours on a mooring buoy for rest and passage planning, instead of taking the soft option in a marina. Why?

Motor yacht work provides a refreshing change for an instructor, but Geoff prefers to deliver sailing yachts.

Because delays give time for worry and also a skipper must be able to cope with stress.

While many Examiners work locally, particularly in the overcrowded Solent, Geoff likes to travel further afield for a change of scenery and new evaluation of the tasks involved. He regularly examines for schools in the south of France and Sardinia, both of which provide a different kind of challenge with the possibility of strong winds and difficult sea conditions during autumn and winter months, despite the advertised image.

One of the obvious downsides of working as an Examiner is having to fail candidates. Geoff says there is a big temptation to be lenient, but examiners have to harden their hearts in order to be correct and fair. Geoff puts the average failure rate at around 15% and has experienced people getting very upset, or even belligerent, when he refuses to sign them off as Yachtmasters. The trick is to find a situation where it's crystal clear why the candidate has failed, with the result that people are sensible and in Geoff's words "take it on the chin" based on their experience. A very few appeal to the RYA, usually because they do not understand the ability level they need to attain.

Expert Witness

Geoff was given his first job as an 'expert witness' in the 1995, when that kind of work was little known. A solicitor asked the RYA to recommend an expert with knowledge of sailing in the English Channel, sailing single-handed and sailing a specific model of yacht. Geoff fitted the bill perfectly, which launched a new aspect to his career.

Geoff's work as an expert witness can range from injuries caused by a rough ride in a RIB, to boats being sunk or crew drowned, people falling off harbour walls or yachts ashore, sometimes with fatal results. Cases can involve a lot of work, but Geoff says it's fascinating, particularly when watching and listening to legal experts.

He may have to give evidence in court, when he will have to justify his opinion when cross-examined by the other side's barrister. ❖

YACHTING
WORKING IN DESIGN and DEVELOPMENT

Yacht design has become highly sophisticated and calls on a wide range of theoretical knowledge and practical 'hands-on' skills. One of Britain's top racing yacht designers explains what is required to succeed in this demanding profession, while a marine electronics specialist explains what it takes to work in R&D…

Seb Josse training on BT Open 60 for the Vendee Globe race, using specially developed equipment by B&G. Photo courtesy navico.com

Offshore Challenges Sailing Team

THE DESIGN DREAM – Simon Rogers

Simon Rogers inside the mould frame for his Artemis IMOCA Open 60 design.

When Simon took the HND, it was run as a sandwich course with work placements for as long as four months each year. This gave Simon the opportunity to work for Rob Humphreys on the design of a round the world racing yacht, gaining practical experience and making useful contacts, which led to a full time job with Humphreys' Yacht Design when Simon qualified.

Unfortunately, that kind of opportunity is no longer so easy to find. Design software has become so complex that Simon reckons it could take a full year before someone can play a productive role in his office. There is no longer any use for just picking up a draughtsman's pen! This means that a work placement student could be disruptive and waste a lot of time, without making any useful contribution. An additional problem is that leading design teams may be involved with confidential projects, making it impossible to admit outsiders.

Rogers Yacht Design (RYD), a well recognised and respected international design office, was founded by Simon and Rebeca Rogers in 1990. Exciting projects developed by RYD range from the Artemis 20 open keelboat to the luxurious Rogers 82 cruiser-racer.

Getting the qualification

Simon Rogers completed the Higher National Diploma in yacht design at the Southampton Institute in 1989, when it was internationally recognised as the best and most specific course available. The modern equivalent is a BEng Honours in Yacht and Powercraft Design at Southampton Solent University, which is still highly recommended by Simon, although he believes it's a great shame there are no longer workshops to provide practical experience.

Get practical experience

If you are determined to become a yacht designer, Simon's advice is "Learn how to build a boat". His view is that too many newly qualified designers have massive theoretical knowledge combined with too little practical knowledge.

The best way to get practical experience is to work in a boatbuilding yard, which has direct involvement with the kind of design team you would like to work for. Design drawings need to be broken into separate components, by copying and pasting, for individual elements of the construction programme.

Artemis IMOCA Open 60, designed by Simon Rogers for the 2008 Vendee Globe.

Simon reckons this kind of opportunity is available for young people who are prepared to work hard and travel anywhere, which makes it ideal for someone straight out of university. However, he cautions that finding work in yard building the latest hi-tech designs will be most difficult, because there are so few around the world. What's more, the transition from boatyard to design office is only likely to result from developing a close working relationship which creates trust – what you can do and who you know are very important.

Surprisingly, Simon says you don't need to be a hot sailor to become a hot designer – in fact you don't need to go sailing at all!

Many leading designers are good sailors, but 'pro race' ability is irrelevant if you don't have the practical and theoretical engineering expertise to produce successful designs.

Making money

After two years of working for Rob Humphreys, Simon decided to set up his own design office, with his wife Rebecca providing marketing and PR skills. The big break came in 1994 when their racing yacht Sticky Fingers turned Rogers Yacht Design into an international name. It was a gamble. Simon and Rebeca had put everything on the line by selling their house to raise enough cash to build and campaign Sticky Fingers.

There is no longer any use for just picking up a draughtsman's pen... a work placement student could be disruptive and waste a lot of time, without making any useful contribution.

The designer works with the builder to create a high performance yacht.

back as soon as the credit crunch began to bite in the autumn of 2008, the 18 month build programme for the Rogers 82 was unaffected. That kind of top league project has a very long lead time, helping to shelter designers and builders from short-term fallout caused by financial markets. Very wealthy people generally provide a stable market, but even if they cut back there is plenty of commercial work for a design team like RYD. For instance, Simon says that 'little jobs' such as a keel and rudder optimisation are always useful, not least because they may create future opportunities to design a complete yacht!

Design ambition

Simon knew he wanted to be a yacht designer from a young age and was totally focused on that ambition. So what advice would he give to anyone with similar ambitions?

Firstly, the importance of being very good at maths and extremely computer literate is increasing all the time. Secondly, you should learn how to build boats as soon as possible – start by refurbishing an old dinghy or building a new dinghy from scratch. Simon emphasises that you also need to get out and work in the marine trade to build up a relationship with people who may help your future career. He started by working at a local boatyard on Saturday mornings. It's an excellent example to follow, even if you have to follow Simon's example by brushing floors and making coffee!

■ www.rogersyachtdesign.com ❖

They recognised that a major financial risk was necessary to get established, but also understood what would happen if things did not work out. Despite producing a stream of famous and extremely successful yachts, the boatbuilding business run by Simon's father Jeremy was bankrupted in the 1980s recession due to lack of cash. The collapse of Contessa Yachts taught Simon that the yacht business can be a very tough game.

More than two decades later, Simon says that the effects of an economic downturn will depend on your market. For instance, while many production yacht builders had to cut

The collapse of Contessa Yachts taught Simon that the yacht business can be a very tough game.

R&D MANAGER – Matt Eeles

Matt develops high performance electronics for B&G. His customers include America's Cup, Volvo 70, Open 60 and Maxi multihull teams…

Matt, can you give us the background to your career and explain what your work involves?

I graduated in 1995 with a degree in Software Engineering & Management, then spent six years working in the industry, followed by an Olympic Tornado campaign that went from part time to full time with lottery funding. My professional sailing finally came to an end in 2003, so I decided to combine my working career with my sailing career. There was one obvious company that captured my interest and allowed me to combine all skills – Brookes & Gatehouse, more commonly known as 'B&G.'

I started as a Software Engineer working in Research & Development, designing and developing software for B&G products. After a short time I fitted in with a set of like-minded colleagues and literally got to know the B&G products inside and out. Today, I still maintain a technical role in the team but also have the responsibility of being R&D Manager. My work is now more varied with the management of an R&D team, which consists of budgets, project plans, new product ideas, custom projects and customer liaison.

Is that a great job?

As a sailor I look forward to work! I spend my week researching and developing our future products and keeping abreast of the latest technology, alongside custom projects for America's Cup teams, Volvo 70s, Open 60s and Maxi Multis. This also involves some on the water testing, customer relations and travel. For example, 2008 was an important year for the Open 60 teams and the Vendee Globe, so we were busy developing and tuning autopilots for the new generation of Open 60s. We also have a good working relationship with the BT Open 60 team as technical partners and we spent a lot of time working with their skipper Seb Josse, testing and tuning the pilot software. Other colleagues are actively involved with Volvo Ocean Race and America's Cup teams, providing technical and regatta support.
It is very satisfying seeing the latest yachts racing around the world and relying on products that the team at B&G has developed. You take on a lot of responsibility to ensure those products do the job well – being a sailor, you understand the requirements.

It is very satisfying seeing the latest yachts racing around the world relying on products that the team at B&G has developed. You take on a lot of responsibility to ensure those products do the job well…

Matt Eeles and his team at B&G developed a custom navstation to enable Seb Josse to race around the world non-stop and single-handed.

How has your career developed over the years? What have been the highlights?

I've been with B&G now for six years and we are a young, enthusiastic group of people with a passion for performance yacht racing. When you have a passion for the products and the industry, your career develops naturally. I did not set out to be an R&D manager, but ended up in my current role because I'm passionate about our products. When you work for a company, you need to be passionate about your career and let the rewards come later.

The highlights are always when I visit a customer and see our products in action, or just walking through a marina and seeing our products on race or cruising yachts. Over the past six years, I've also been lucky enough to go sailing on some high profile boats, most recently, the RC44 Gold Cup in Lanzarote when I sailed with Russell Coutts and Dean Barker, while providing electronics support.

How would you rate the importance of academic qualifications, compared to sailing and regatta experience, for the kind of work you do at B&G?

Within R&D, degree qualifications along with an inquisitive mind and technical knowledge of sailing are all desirable. We would look for a degree qualification in electronics, software, physics or mathematics with an emphasis on software, control and instrumentation. When you get involved in writing specifications, talking to customers or testing products, a level of racing experience is also necessary. This means you can communicate with customers at their level of sailing and respond in a professional and knowledgeable manner. It is something we have found hard to recruit for because not everyone loves sailing – in fact our current long-term employees have all been recruited from networking.

It seems that electronics and IT are fundamental to modern yachts. Does that mean there are good career opportunities?

Our customers are relying more and more on instrumentation and control systems. Custom boats designed to break records or win races need accurate instrumentation to monitor and control the boat. This trend can only increase and get more complex as the boats get bigger and faster, with all the technology filtering down through grand prix and regatta race boats.

To be involved, you do not need to be in R&D developing products. Technical support or regatta support is very much a key activity in supporting our products. Generally, these people are the ones who build up the good relationships with our customers, ready to fly around the world at short notice or talk on the phone to a skipper in the middle of the night, giving technical support for a race boat in the Southern Ocean. But these people all have one thing in common. They have a technical electrical or software background and are sailors with a passion for performance racing.

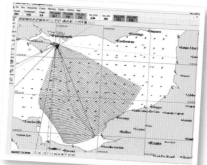
Screen routing design by B&G.

Is there any danger that all this hard work might ruin your love of the sport?

I feel very privileged to be involved with our customers and projects, particularly when that customer is a single-handed sailor racing in the Vendee Globe or a team in the Volvo Ocean Race. You don't think of it as hard work! Our customers are sometimes our friends and we have a duty to support them by providing safe and reliable instrumentation and autopilots. It is hard to imagine this kind of work could ruin the sport for me! The projects and customers are varied and constantly expand my understanding of the sport. It also gives me the opportunities to enjoy many different types of sailing.

Have you any plans to change your sailing or career in the years ahead?

My sailing has always been focused on racing multihulls, which has allowed me to experience some great sailing in great conditions.

But between jobs in 2000, I took some time out and cruised on a yacht with three friends from Malaysia to Crete via the Red Sea. We visited nine countries, remote islands and met some fascinating people cruising in small boats on small budgets. I loved the adventure and the mode of travel and it showed me a different side to sailing. So at some point I would love to sell up and do a cruising circumnavigation. My work has allowed me to develop the systems that one day I hope to use for navigation, safety and monitoring my own yacht! ❖

Technical support or regatta support is very much a key activity in supporting our products... these people are the ones who build up the good relationships with our customers...

SOUTHAMPTON SOLENT UNIVERSITY

Southampton Solent University (formerly the Southampton Institute) has trained many graduates who have gone on to achieve great success in yacht design and associated fields. The university runs two courses with an international reputation. Career opportunities include working in yacht design and naval architect offices, technical management of new construction, design and production engineering, composite specialist work, classification societies, production and management, project management and surveying positions, marine equipment design and manufacture.

BEng (Hons) Yacht and Powercraft Design   3 years full time.

■ If you're interested in sailing and boating, and are keen to become a yacht designer, then this respected engineering degree could be ideal. With over 30 years of experience, this is the world's leading course in Yacht and Powercraft Design. It covers practical design work whilst underpinning theory.

■ Delivered by highly qualified, award-winning staff, this course maintains close links with the yacht and small craft industry. Indeed, with extensive design experience on tap, you'll emerge as a graduate with the analytical and design skills of a naval architect.

■ The course seeks to complement your existing practical sailing and boatcraft knowledge, and combines theory and practice in an ideal location. Southampton Solent University is close to the thriving Port of Southampton and its successful business community, and is therefore a superb place for extra practical experience. You'll gain access to industry-standard facilities in the City Centre and Warsash Maritime Academy, where you can develop design skills using computer aided design (CAD) and participate in practical workshops. In towing and stability tanks, labs and Fibre Reinforced Plastic (FRP) workshops, you'll also get to cover the manufacture of composites, material testing, stability and marine engine investigations.

■ The professionally recognised BEng (Hons) Yacht and Powercraft Design degree is one of the world's leading courses, fully accredited by the Royal Institution of Naval Architects.

ASSESSMENT

■ Most units are assessed through a combination of course work, assignments, design briefs, build and test projects, group work and presentations. Some units are assessed through end-unit examinations.
■ The Project is assessed through the final dissertation and associated CAD-generated drawings.

ENTRY LEVEL

■ 180 points from two or more numerically based A Levels or equivalent.
■ Entry may be offered to applicants holding an HND in an appropriate subject. This course is also available with a Technology Foundation Year. There are different UCAS codes for the main degree and the degree with a Foundation Year.

BEng (Hons) Yacht Production and Surveying

3 years full time.

■ BEng (Hons) Yacht Production and Surveying is for yacht technologists, with an emphasis on the more practical considerations of production, manufacture and surveying. The degree shares some units with the BEng (Hons) Yacht and Powercraft Design; both provide a good grounding in Computer-aided Drawing (CAD), and practical experience of modern construction materials and methods. The three principal themes running through all three years are: Yacht Materials and Manufacture; Yacht Safety Assessment; Yacht Design Technology.

■ This technology degree aims to produce graduates with the project management, numerical and practical skills of a professional Marine Technologist working in the yacht industry. You undertake a programme of lectures and tutorials. Supporting workshops include practical exercises on manufacture of composites, material testing, stability and marine engine investigations. These are carried out using the University's towing and stability tanks, material testing laboratories and FRP workshops.

Entry level
■ 180 points from two or more numerically based A levels or equivalent.
■ Entry may be offered to applicants holding an HND in an appropriate subject. This course is also available with a Technology Foundation year.

More information:
Faculty of Technology – Engineering, Construction and Maritime Group.
Tel: 023 80319141
Email: ft.admissions@solent.ac.uk
■ **www.solent.ac.uk**

POWERBOATING INSTRUCTOR 12

The rapid growth in powerboats, from high speed RIBs to large motor yachts, has created great opportunities for teaching private and commercial users how to handle powercraft confidently and safely...

RYA CHIEF POWERBOAT INSTRUCTOR
– Paul Mara

RYA

Paul, can you tell us how your career led to working for the RYA?

I was introduced to powerboating in the 1980s, initially volunteering as safety boat crew at an RYA training centre. As time passed I accumulated powerboating qualifications, passing my instructor course in 1992. For many years I worked as a part-time freelance instructor on the east coast and on the tidal Thames in London. In 1999, the largest passenger carrier approached me on the Thames to write Domestic Ship Safety Management systems for their fleet of tourist boats, which took three years. When it ended, I was contracted as Marine Safety Advisor by British Airways London Eye, setting up their safety management procedures on Waterloo Pier.

During all this commercial work, I still found time to continue my small boat activity and also found a lot of work in the TV and film industry, driving camera boats and action boats for programmes such as Ultimate Force, The Lost Prince and live news reports. In 2002 I was approached by Channel 4 to be the judge in an

episode of Scrapheap Challenge. The same year I went to Malta for many months, working on the set of the Hollywood hit Troy – my duties included supporting the marine co-ordinator in managing the safety of up to three hundred people on the water.

After returning from Malta I decided to set up my own RYA training centre on the River Medway in Kent, providing training to the general public and professional operators. Having qualified as a Powerboat Trainer and subsequently becoming an inspector of training centres, I was sent to New Zealand to assist my predecessor in setting up the RYA training programme for the New Zealand Coastguard. I then joined the RYA in 2005.

What does your job at the RYA involve?

The main focus of my job is to maintain tuition and safety standards at RYA powerboat training centres. Currently there are approximately 1,300 powerboat centres in 23 countries worldwide, each of which has to be inspected on an annual basis. We have a team of freelance inspectors who fulfil this role. In addition I am responsible for training and updating our Powerboat Trainers and Examiners.

Another aspect is to investigate powerboat accidents at RYA training centres, sometimes assisting the Marine Accident Investigation Branch and the Maritime and Coastguard Agency when they require specialist advice. For instance, I investigated a boating fatality on behalf of the Procurator Fiscal in Scotland, which required me to produce a lengthy report and give evidence in court. I have a full time PA to keep me on the straight and narrow, who is invaluable as my work takes me away from the office for a large part of my time. Strangely enough, these days I spend very little time afloat!

Teaching boat handling skills has widespread applications.

RYA

What kind of skills and temperament are required for someone who wants to work as a powerboat instructor? What qualifications are vital or desirable?

To become an RYA powerboat instructor you need to hold RYA Powerboat Level 2 certificate and have five seasons of powerboating experience. You will have to pass skills assessment and then attend a three-day instructor course. Successful candidates would be good communicators, technically competent and must be enthusiastic about the subject.

Do you get situations where powerboat instructors fail to match the required standards and may risk losing their qualification?

Unfortunately, one of the least enjoyable parts of the job is putting together a disciplinary case against an instructor. But at the end of the day, if withdrawal of an instructor's qualification is necessary it can only be for the greater good of the training program.

What kind of job opportunities are available for people who want to work as powerboat instructors?

Some people make a full-time living out of being a powerboat instructor, but many are multi-disciplined so they are more attractive to training centres.

Are you responsible for alternative powerboat instruction, such as personal watercraft and inland waterways?

Yes, both the PW and Inland Waterways schemes and also the new PW Training on Superyachts course. It's worth mentioning that there is less opportunity to gain full-time employment in these fields.

What advice would you give to a young person who is coming up to leaving school and wants to work with powerboats?

Join a club and learn the ropes as a safety boat operator. Gain the basic qualifications and then log every hour spent on a powerboat, while working towards your instructor award. ❖

QUALIFYING AS AN RYA POWERBOAT INSTRUCTOR

Powerboat Instructor

Minimum Age: 16

■ **Essential requirements:** At least five seasons' experience of powerboating, or one season as full time work; RYA Level 2 powerboat certificate; First Aid certificate; RYA powerboat instructor skills test.

■ **Useful qualifications:** SRC radio certificate; RYA Dayskipper shorebased; RYA Safety Boat; RYA Intermediate and Advanced powerboat certificate .

A Powerboat Instructor is a competent, experienced powerboater who has been trained to teach powerboating up to Level 2 under the supervision of the Principal or Chief Instructor of a recognised centre. Powerboat instructors with safety boat certificate may run the safety boat course at a recognised training centre. Candidates must complete a Skills Assessment, which lasts approximately half a day or a full day with preparation. The Powerboat Instructor course is held over three days and assessed by an independent trainer. The course includes principles of practical instruction, lesson planning, teaching styles, use of questioning, preparation and use of visual aids, assessment of students' learning, explanation and presentation of theory subjects, the structure of the scheme, planning progressive teaching sessions, preparation of boats and equipment and teaching methods to Level 2.

Advanced Power Instructor
Minimum Age: 17

■ **Essential requirements:** RYA Powerboat Level 2 coastal and advanced powerboat certificates; RYA powerboat instructor skills test; SRC radio certificate.

■ **Useful qualifications:** Sea Survival; RYA Dayskipper shorebased; RYA Safety Boat.

An Advanced Powerboat Instructor has been trained to teach intermediate and advanced courses, coaching experienced drivers and teaching the practical night navigation exercise. The course is held over two days and assessed by an independent RYA powerboat trainer. A commercially endorsed advanced powerboat certificate is required to teach the advanced course on board a boat that is subject to MCA codes of practice.

BSAC Boat Handling Instructor

Minimum Age: 18

■ **Essential requirements:** First Aid certificate; RYA Powerboat Level 2 coastal certificate; BSAC Diver Cox'n; RYA Powerboat Instructor.

■ **Useful qualifications:** SRC radio certificate; RYA Dayskipper shorebased; RYA Advanced Powerboat certificate.

One day endorsement course for RYA Powerboat Instructors who wish to teach BSAC courses.

BSAC Diver Cox'n Assessor

Minimum Age: 18

■ **Essential requirements:** First Aid certificate; RYA Powerboat Level 2 coastal certificate; BSAC Diver Cox'n; BSAC Boat Handling Instructor; RYA Powerboat Instructor.

■ **Useful qualifications:** SRC radio certificate; RYA Dayskipper shorebased; RYA Advanced Powerboat certificate.

One day endorsement course for BSAC Boat Handling Instructors.

Inland Waterways Instructor

Minimum Age: 18

■ **Essential requirements:** Inland Waterways Helmsman's certificate; First Aid certificate with emphasis on hypothermia and resuscitation; Marine Radio Operator's Short Range Certificate; maxmum age limit of 65 years.

An Inland Waterways Instructor is expected to have extensive experience on inland waters of the UK. The one day instructor course may take place on canals or rivers, using both a narrowboat and cruiser. It is designed to develop instructional technique and ensure that teaching will be done to the required standard.

BOAT TRAINING WITH THE MET
– Steve Ingamells

An opportunity to join the River Police gave Steve Ingamells the training and experience to open his own powerboat school…

I joined the Metropolitan Police force in 1978 at the age of 18 and kept my feet firmly on the shore, doing many aspects of police work in London. Thirty years service is quite enough for anyone and I was able to retire at the age of 48! Eight years before that happened, I knew I had to do something different within the police service to take me towards my next job after retirement.

In December 1999 I noticed there were vacancies in the Marine Support Unit on the River Thames. A close of friend of mine already worked on the unit and was able to give me an idea what the job was about. I liked what I heard and applied along with 80 other officers for six places. Luckily, I was accepted, joined

in February 2000 and stayed on the unit until I retired in 2008. Marine Support work is very varied and is now mainly concentrated on anti-terrorism, but is also responsible for body recovery on the Thames and any waterway within the London area. The unit provides 24-hour patrols in London and deals with all crime matters on the river and public order issues on central London party boats. Working with the River Police is extremely interesting and I would recommend it to any police officer, providing they knew what to expect.

Moving on
During my time with the River Police, I managed to meet many river users including the principal of a powerboat school. I became a very good friend and managed to get the RYA powerboat instructor course under my belt, whilst working as a police officer. About three years before I retired from the police, I heard that Guardian powerboat school was for sale. This was the avenue I wanted to take upon retirement, so I decided to buy it!

The work
Guardian offers all powerboat courses. As I am a trainer, I also run instructor courses for Power and PWC (jet ski), with many customers coming from the commercial sector. Requirements will differ. We cover the RYA powerboat scheme, but some courses will be tailor-made for commercial operators and not come within the remit of the RYA. Other courses that we run include VHF Radio, First Aid and shore based courses up to Yachtmaster.

Marine Support work is very varied and is now mainly concentrated on anti-terrorism, but is also responsible for body recovery on the Thames…

An instructor must be patient, knowledgeable, confident and adaptable, as well as being a role model...

Steve got an opportunity to work afloat in the Police, which led to running his own powerboat school.

The skills

Skills required for a good instructor are endless, but must include the promotion of safety, which is paramount. An instructor must be patient, knowledgeable, confident and adaptable, as well as being a role model to name but a few attributes – I could list 30 or 40 more!

The qualifications

To become an instructor, you must hold a Level 2 Powerboat certificate, RYA First Aid certificate or equivalent, and have experience on the water. Within the RYA scheme, we now have an assessment prior to the student coming on the course.

The earnings

A powerboat school will not provide sufficient income through just teaching people. Your boat needs to be working as much as possible, but no one wants to be in an open boat in the middle of winter. The overheads can be massive and a lot of effort and passion are needed to earn a decent income. Stressful, yes! But the best times are when business is busy and the worst times are when enquiries stop.

Words of wisdom

Powerboat instruction is not easy to develop as a career. Do it, enjoy it and be safe, but don't expect to earn much money from it!

■ www.boattraining.co.uk

SPECIALIST IN POWERBOAT TRAINING
– Jon Mendez

J on Mendez, formerly chief motor and powerboat instructor at the RYA, runs Mendez Marine with the specific objective of providing high quality powerboat training…

Jon, how did you get involved with powerboat training?

Bought a boat, having had a few years away from the water. Loved it again, was chatting to a Sea School skipper and the penny dropped – I could play boats for a living!

What services does Mendez Marine provide?

RYA training courses, delivery of craft, specialist own-boat tuition and we also work with commercial users including police and navy.

What are the best and worst things about your job?

The hardest part is getting customers and then matching them to dates that suit everyone. It's pretty competitive, so you have to be really customer focused.

Is work experience available with Mendez Marine?

'Assistants' often come along to gain mileage experience for their qualifications. We have also looked at an 'apprentice' scheme and hope to follow that route.

What kind of skills and temperament are required to work as a powerboat instructor?

Without doubt the key skill is patience and the ability to get along with other people. It also helps if you can actually drive the boat! In addition, you'll need qualifications through the RYA instructor scheme.

What advice would you give to a young person who is coming up to leaving school and wants to work with powerboats?

One of the best routes is without doubt through your local club. Learn to sail as well, because it's a great help. Get qualified at a basic level, and then consider working at one of the big holiday clubs like Sunsail, where you will gain a good insight into the industry and be able to gauge if you are sufficiently customer-focused. The superyacht industry could be another good route, but they all require HARD work. If you just want to play – forget it!

Any advice you would like to add?

Yep, it's simple really. Work hard, watch what goes on, and look for a role model or mentor. There are many mistakes to make, so learn from someone who has already made most of them!

■ www.mendezmarine.co.uk   ❖

Work hard, watch what goes on, and look for a role model or mentor. There are many mistakes to make, so learn from someone who has already made most of them!

RYA

PERSONAL WATER CRAFT

Would you like to work with PWCs, better known as jetskis? Candi Abbott, Director of the Personal Watercraft Partnership, explains the opportunities and excitement linked to teaching people how to handle this ultra-fast sector of marine sport.

www.jetmanuk.com

Candi, how did you become involved with the PWP?

Having worked in the industry as a freelance RYA instructor (Dinghy, Powerboat, PW) since I was 18 and set up and run an RYA Powerboat & PWC recognised centre for seven years, I sold up in January 2008 to try and have a 'change of scene'. I wasn't looking to change my industry but rather to broaden my experience. I applied for the PWP director's position as throughout my career I was consistently witnessing problems with PWCs all over the country and hearing a negative response. I didn't actually get the job first time round, which I later found out was because the interview panel was concerned about whether I would find it 'interesting enough', but when the position re-opened in October 2008 I was the first one at the door!

Is that an interesting career? Can you describe your day-to-day work?

It's probably not a career choice for everyone, but is interesting because my work is so diverse. That is exactly what I was looking for after I sold my school – another challenge! I am employed on a part-time (3 days a week) basis and

therefore have the opportunity to focus on PWP issues in addition to continuing with freelance RYA instruction and other jobs like working with RYA Volvo Champion Clubs and Sailability.

My day to day work can range from not so exciting administration to meetings with MP's, councils, harbour authorities or marine police to discuss management of PWCs in their specific areas. Along with this, the PWP are heavily involved with clubs and therefore I get to spend time on and off the water with club committees and members.

What kind of job opportunities are available for someone who wants to work as a PWC instructor? Is there much work for holiday/gap year instructors? How easily can it be developed as a full-time career?

There are plenty of opportunities for people looking to work as a PWC instructor along with any other area of teaching on the water (dinghy, windsurf, powerboat, etc). I would say it is based not only on your skill and range of qualifications, but also very heavily on your personality. If you teach a group of students at a centre and have synergy with them, they are more likely to enjoy and retain the skills and information you give during the course. In the long-term, this is not only positive for them but also the safety of everyone else on the water. Also, it gives a good image to the sport, the RYA and you as their instructor. The more positive feedback you get from your students, the more offers of work will come your way!

My day to day work can range from not so exciting administration to meetings with MPs, councils, harbour authorities or marine police to discuss management of PWCs in their specific areas.

Getting wet goes with the job – Candi goes to work at the Yamaha 50th Anniversary Event.

With regard to holiday/gap year instructors, there are plenty of opportunities to teach in the UK and abroad. If sun, sea and sand are your thing, then head for one of the overseas operators like Neilson, Sunsail, Mark Warner or Crystal Active who are always looking for instructors to work for summer seasons. You are much more likely to get a job if you have a range of qualifications – for instance dinghy and windsurf instructor, along with a safety boat certificate. This makes you a more desirable candidate as you can cover all aspects of activities that the holiday companies offer.

If you don't want to go abroad, clubs and centres in the UK also have plenty on offer, with many multi-activity centres (council and privately run) that focus on summer work. Once again, if you are looking at working a full-time season at a multi-activity centre then a range of disciplines will be far more desirable. However, there are some opportunities for working at discipline-specific centres such as RYA powerboat schools.

Developing your teaching into a full-time career is purely a case of how dedicated you are to developing your own skills, along with commitment to your sports and the centre you are working at. If you work a season at an RYA teaching establishment, it is the commitment of the centre to offer you further training. Whether this is at the beginning, end or during your season will be specific to the centre, but if you show commitment and a likeliness to return the following year, then they should encourage your development. For instance, you could start work at a centre as an assistant dinghy instructor (working alongside a Senior dinghy instructor) and complete your dinghy instructor qualification during the same season. You can then expand into other areas like catamaran or keelboat instruction or perhaps move up to a group management role like Senior Instructor.

PWCs play an important role for rescue and patrols, using highly trained drivers.

What about commercial work using PWCs for emergency services or high-speed patrols? That sounds interesting, but what kind of opportunities are available?

The use of PWCs in a commercial environment has been on the increase over the last few years. Beach and surf rescue teams, harbour patrols, marine police and other safety organisations now actively use them. In the USA they are used for big surf rescue and tow-in surfing. This is having some impact on the UK scene, where PWCs are in use at some kitesurfing and windsurfing competitions, acting as rescue craft due to their handling and manoeuvrability in difficult environments.

What advice would you give to someone would like to work with PWCs? What are good ways to get started, considering all the different kinds of jobs that might be available?

For a recent school leaver, I would focus on getting into a school as an assistant instructor on the basis that the school will help train you and put you through RYA qualifications. By working alongside experienced instructors you will not only have the opportunity to develop your personal skills but also observe a wide variety of teaching methods in an active environment.

If finances provide, it is also possible to attend the kind of intensive training course that

The use of PWCs in a commercial environment has been on the increase over the last few years...

companies like UKSA and Flying Fish offer. For example, if your sport skills are limited you can join a 'core skills training course' to develop skills in your chosen discipline up to the standard required to attend an instructor course. Assuming you successfully pass this, you can apply to work at a centre or do an 'Instructor development course'. This offers the opportunity to start teaching in a structured environment where experienced senior instructors are 'on tap' to give advice, support and feedback, with opportunities to upgrade your basic qualification and gain experience in other aspects of working at a large centre.

The qualification for teaching PWCs at RYA centres is the RYA PWC instructor certificate. This is a 3-day course that is offered to anyone holding the RYA PWC competency and first aid certificate, but a good amount of handling experience is required prior to completing the course. Another career route could be harbour patrol on a PWC through a local harbour masters office. Qualifications required for this are usually RYA PWC competency, first aid and VHF certificate. Or you could try working on the beach with lifeguards!

...beach and surf rescue teams, harbour patrols, marine police and other safety organisations now actively use them.

Any advice you would like to add?

Beware! When I was 18, I trained as an instructor in order to work a couple of summers on the water whilst I decided what degree to do at university. It is now 10 years on. I never did go to uni and am still full-time in the watersports industry. I wouldn't change a thing. The combination of being passionate about what I do and some hard work has given me the opportunity to advance through the qualifications in dinghy sailing, powerboating and PWC and get to a stage where I can teach complete beginners all the way through to instructors and commercial operators. The added bonus, which has been a huge influence, is that I have had the opportunity to travel the world from Europe to the Middle East and Southern Hemisphere. My family was initially disappointed that I didn't go to uni. But now they can see what a massive amount of life experience I have gained, not only from the diversity of people I have met and places I have been, but also from running a successful company for many years. Depending on the direction you wish to take in life, that combination can surely match, if not beat, a university degree?

■ www.pwpuk.org   ❖

QUALIFYING AS AN RYA PERSONAL WATERCRAFT INSTRUCTOR

Minimum Age: 16

■ **Essential requirements:** First Aid certificate; RYA personal watercraft proficiency certificate; at least two years' experience of driving personal watercraft.

■ **Useful qualifications:** SRC radio certificate; RYA Powerboat Level 2 certificate.

Personal watercraft (PW) instructors have been trained and assessed to run the RYA's Personal Watercraft Proficiency course. PW instructors can also run the RYA's Introduction to PW Safety course for guests on superyacht holidays. The instructor course is run over three days by a PW trainer and assessed by an independent trainer. Alternatively, qualified powerboat instructors may take a one day conversion course.

14

WORKING AS AN RYA SHOREBASED INSTRUCTOR

Many of the courses offered by the RYA are shore-based, providing instruction at Day Skipper, Coastal Skipper/Yachtmaster Offshore and Yachtmaster Ocean level, alongside shorter courses including radio procedure, radar, sea survival and first aid. These can provide instructors with a useful addition to working on water, particularly during the winter!

Jeremy Evans

Sunsail

Teaching in a Sunsail classroom before going afloat. Theory plays a major role in RYA yachting qualifications, ensuring that students can manage tides and weather systems.

CR MARINE TRAINING – Colin Ridley

Colin, can you give us the background to your sailing career? What have been the highlights and major breaks?

I first went sailing when I left school. A friend took me out on his Fireball dinghy and I was hooked. Two weeks later I had my own Fireball, which I learnt to sail in a winter series at my local sailing club. In retrospect this isn't an approach I would recommend to newcomers wanting to learn to sail! However, that was the start and two decades of club and open meeting racing with a Laser provided loads more experience.

I also got involved with the local Sea Cadets and teaching youngsters to sail. Wanting to do this properly, I went on an RYA Dinghy Instructor course and saw a totally different side of sailing. For self improvement I then went on further RYA courses, including a variety of RYA instructor level courses. So my list of qualifications has been based around experience.

The highlights have been the first day I went on my friend's Fireball, followed by my introduction to teaching youngsters to sail on dinghies and yachts. Being made redundant from a position as an IT Project Manager was the best break ever, as it allowed me to turn a hobby into a career! More recently, being awarded the RYA Instructor of the Year award in 2008 was a highlight that I'm very proud of, as was being asked to co-author the Powerboat Instructor Handbook for the RYA.

What happens at CR Marine Training?

After being made redundant, I decided to become self employed and develop something that until then had been a leisure activity. Whilst working as an IT Project Manager, many of my holidays involved running courses for a small number of companies and it was these companies that provided the first opportunities for proper work as an instructor. My range of qualifications meant I was also able to set up my own RYA Training Centre – CR Marine Training – and get RYA recognition for all the shorebased courses I can teach. This has provided further work opportunities and the intended income stream.

How many aspects of yachting are you qualified to teach? What kind of skills and temperament are required?

My qualifications are quite extensive, but in each case I've always made sure I have experience in the area before becoming an instructor.

To teach courses successfully, I never forget that the students are learning and will not always get things right first time. Patience is essential and being 'human' is a key skill requirement!

The list includes Powerboat Trainer, Advanced Powerboat Examiner, Dinghy Coach/Assessor and Yachtmaster Instructor (Sail), which basically qualifies me to teach virtually all dinghy, powerboat and yachting courses including theory to Ocean Yachtmaster, as well as one day courses including Sea Survival, SRC/VHF, First Aid and the ISAF Offshore Safety Course (First Aid, Sea Survival and Offshore Safety for long distance races such as the Fastnet and Sydney-Hobart). I'm also a part-time Sailing Master on a tall ship and a part-time Mate on a 24 metre motor cruiser, both involving sea training for young people in the 12 to 18 age group.

To teach courses successfully, I never forget that the students are learning and will not always get things right first time. Patience is essential and being 'human' is a key skill requirement! Working as a self-employed instructor, you also need to be self-sufficient and spot an opportunity for what it offers.

Shorebased courses get plenty of customers right through the year.

What kind of work pleases you the most? Do you prefer skippering, teaching or running a shorebased course?

Because I can teach so many courses, I'm often asked which one I like best. My usual answer is the one I'm doing at that moment, and that is actually quite truthful because I get involved and therefore enjoy what I'm doing – always making that course the best one! But given a choice of a course to teach I'd probably pick Sea Survival – it's a 1 day course with a mix of theory and practical and could save someone's life. I actually went on a Marine Safety Instructor course in Alaska to further my knowledge on the topic!

People complain that shorebased evening courses, such as day skipper or yachtmaster theory, can be very boring. Is it a challenge to make them interesting?

The image that evening classes can be boring has been around for many years, but is largely incorrect. Like me, many shorebased instructors are also practical boaters so can put a practical slant on a theory course. I always find out about each person on my course in order to make the course more personal for them – for instance are they interested in powerboats or yachts?

Back to basics. Colin provides personal tuition for each student with chart and plotter.

For the course delivery, I try to make each individual evening session develop from an earlier topic when this is possible. I also maintain my own website through which students can check aspects of their answers to homework, as well as the topics covered if they have missed an evening.

What advice, in terms of getting the right experience and qualifications and choosing the best job, would you give to someone who wants to develop a career based on working on water?

It's probably fair to say that you need an instructor qualification as a minimum and then being good at what you do will be the key to opening doors. You don't just need to be an instructor – you need to be a good one! That is likely to come about through your level of enthusiasm and responsibility.

That's the start, then there are opportunities and your own ability to spot and take them! I can think of more than one person I met on their dinghy instructor course, following their first season abroad as an unqualified 'beach assistant,' who are now respected senior managers for that company. They have got there by being good at each role and have been presented with opportunities for advancement. Others have made that start and moved to another company to develop their interests.

For instance, I know a former instructor who progressed to being sales director for a major boat parts distribution business. So the message is "Get qualified, be good, follow your interests and opportunities".

Would you recommend instructing as part-time work or a full-time career?

Working as a sailing instructor for the summer or gap year is a very realistic option. That type of instructor fills most of the summer vacancies of overseas holiday companies and many sailing centres in the UK. For the right people this can become a career, but they will generally have more than one qualification or work with the same company for several years to become a part of the permanent crew. If you want to make it a full-time career, a wide range of high level qualifications is a big help.

What are the best and worst aspects of teaching people about sailing?

The best aspect of teaching people to sail is seeing their pleasure in learning a new skill, which often they knew nothing about. The worst aspect has got to be recognizing that sometimes students need more time to complete a course than is available, with the result that they don't pass. No one likes telling a student that they cannot have their certificate, but we have to accept that passing RYA courses should be based on performance rather than attendance.

Any regrets?

My biggest regret is not being made redundant earlier!

■ www.colinridley.co.uk   ❖

Shorebased Instructor

■ **Essential requirements:** RYA/MCA Yachtmaster Offshore certificate of competence.

The two-day shorebased instructor course is for anyone wanting to teach the RYA's shorebased navigation and seamanship courses – Day Skipper, Coastal Skipper/Yachtmaster Offshore and Yachtmaster Ocean. All applicants must be active cruising or offshore skippers and have successfully completed the Coastal Skipper/Yachtmaster Offshore shorebased course in the last five years. Advanced Powerboat Instructors can also apply, but will only be qualified to teach the Day Skipper shorebased course.

SRC Assessor

■ **Essential requirements:** VHF short range certificate; RYA qualified instructor in discipline such as shorebased, cruising, powerboat or dinghy.

The Short Range Certificate assessor courses are for anyone wanting to teach the RYA's marine radio short range certificate course. SRC assessor courses are organised on a regional basis.

Diesel Instructor

■ **Essential requirements:** Good knowledge of the operation and maintenance of marine diesel engines, including direct and indirect marine cooling systems and salt water filtration. The RYA diesel instructor course takes one day and is mandatory for anyone who wants to teach the RYA's specialist diesel engine maintenance course, which also lasts one day.

Sea Survival Instructor

■ **Essential requirements:** RYA cruising instructor (or higher) or advanced powerboat instructor; Sea Survival Course certificate.

The sea survival course is one of the RYA's specialist one-day courses. The sea survival instructor course lasts four days and is heavily subscribed.

Radar Instructor

■ **Essential requirements:** Experienced in the use of small marine radar with knowledge well in excess of the RYA's radar course.

The RYA radar instructor course takes one day and is mandatory for anyone who wants to teach the RYA's specialist radar course, which also lasts one day.

First Aid Instructor

■ **Essential requirements:** HSE First Aid at Work certificate or equivalent; doctors and nurses with recent appropriate acute experience and paramedics are exempt from the need for a first aid certificate, but must be aware of current first aid practices as detailed in the Red Cross/St Johns/St Andrews First Aid Manual; VHF or SRC certificate.

■ **Useful qualifications:** RYA instructor in another field; RYA Sea Survival.

The first aid course is one of the RYA's specialist one-day courses. In order to teach it you must qualify as an RYA first aid instructor. Instructors must appreciate the restrictions of first aid in the marine environment, which makes boating experience essential.

WORKING IN THE MEDIA 15

Journalism and photography can provide two exciting ways to work on water, either with the security of working for a large company or the freedom of being self-employed. You could even try TV as well…

Always looking for new angles. A view from the water by top yachting photographer Richard Langdon.

Ocean Images

OCEAN IMAGES – Richard Langdon

Ocean Images

Richard Langdon specialises in yacht and dinghy photography, working for clients that include the RYA Skandia Olympic Team.

Richard, what is the best way to get started in your profession?

I would recommend studying photography before embarking on a serious career in sailing photography. My course was at Bournemouth and Poole College of Art and Design.

When and why did you decide to specialise in yachting photography?

I left college in 1988 and had no regular income, so decided to give it a go straight away. I was always a keen sailor.

Does yachting photography have a lot in common with other types of professional photography?

I guess the nearest style would be other sports photography, but a lot depends on how the photographer wants to approach the subject and what he or she wants to achieve.

Did you get any major career breaks?

I can't pinpoint one event that got my career going. It's just a case of starting and letting the results speak for themselves.

What are the best aspects and work aspects of working as a professional yachting photographer?

Working on the water is great. To combine that with something I love is fantastic.

What have been the most memorable shoots you have done?

I'm lucky. There are too many to mention! A few would be an Atlantic crossing on a Volvo 60, ice sailing and a day out on the foiling trimaran L'Hydroptere.

Things must go wrong. What is the worst shoot you have ever done?

Flying to cover the Kenwood Cup in Hawaii as freelance work. I chose the only year with a tropical cyclone. The weather was so bad I gave up after 48 hours and flew home!

How much do you travel in a typical year?

I do a lot of travelling each year. On a busy year I will be away approaching half the time.

It sounds like a great lifestyle, but is it a good way to earn an income?

Once established, yes.

Can you tell us how you earn your money?

About 90% of my work is commissioned, approximately split into 50% race coverage and 50% brochures, editorial and other commercial work. My freelance work has to be very selective and either financially or artistically rewarding!

Has digital photography been a bonus for you?

It's changed the job completely and passed on certain tasks to the photographer.

Do you spend a lot of time on image manipulation? How important are those kind of skills?

One day on the water results in at least a day working on the images. Not everything is manipulation as pictures also need captioning, editing and managing. It is essential to know how to work on the images and exactly what the client wants.

As a photographer, what qualities have made you successful? For instance how much is down to having the right equipment, knowing how to use it, looking for opportunities, being in the right place at the right time and understanding what is happening on the water?

All of these things are important. It's certainly not about buying the best equipment and expecting miracles. Being reliable, so you will get the shots that are expected (and hopefully not expected), as well as getting on with your clients, is very important.

What about organising and marketing your images and making sure you get paid? How do you run that side of the business?

Running the administrative side of Ocean Images is very important. It's another full-time job for more than one person. My wife Marie is on top of all these aspects of the business.

If someone wants to get started as a marine photographer, what equipment do they need to invest in? Could you suggest a 'yachting photographer pro kit on a budget' and a 'pro kit with unlimited cash'?

BUDGET KIT: 2 x Canon EOS5Ds; 1 x Canon 16-35mm f2.8L; 1 x Canon 80-200mm f2.8L; 1 x Canon 300mm f2.8L; 1 x Canon flash

UNLIMITED CASH KIT: 2 x Canon 1DS mkIIIs; 1 x Canon 16-35mm f2; 1 x Canon 24-70mm f2.8L; 1 x Canon 80-

Ocean Images

It is essential to know how to work on the images and exactly what the client wants.

200mm f2.8L; 1 x Canon 300mm f2.8L; 1 x Canon 500mm f4L; 1 x Canon 800mm f5.6L

If a young person at school or college would like to follow a similar kind of career, what tips would you give them?

Have a go! Know the sport well and be prepared for a tough first few years.

Any regrets?
None.

■ **www.oceanimages.co.uk**   ❖

EDITOR AT YACHTS AND YACHTING
Gael Pawson

What are the best things about being editor of Yachts and Yachting?

Editing a sailing magazine is a challenging, varied and rewarding job. I get to meet some amazing people and sometimes sail really interesting boats, but like any job there are boring bits with a lot of long hours and very hard work. It's very satisfying to see an issue in print – especially a bumper issue like our Olympic Games report, when a lot of late nights go into ensuring it gets done in time.

What are the worst things about your job?

I spend more time in front of a computer than people might think. A lot of my job is about organising material, who is going to write it, making sure it arrives on time, is 'subbed' (corrected or rewritten and correctly laid out). We are constantly working to a deadline – the whole thing has to be at the printers or we miss our slot. Sometimes, you really wish there had been more time to work on a feature. One of the worst things is seeing an error slip through, or a feature with amazing photographs but not enough pages to make the most of them.

What would you rate as the most rewarding types of work on water?

Editing a magazine has to be right up there, particularly when you get enthusiastic feedback!

Coaching can be a rewarding career, as you get to bring out the best in someone and can look forward to seeing them achieve.

Yachting photographers have a cool job, especially the top ones who can employ people to sort their shots while they do all the shooting. Sailing is a very challenging sport to photograph. You have to contend with weather, light and sea, as well as everything else, but can get spectacular material.

Live commentary for television or radio can be very exciting, although it's not as easy as you might imagine with many hours of hard work required to make very short pieces.

Yacht restoration seems to be a rewarding area to work in, especially when restoring a traditional craft to its former glory, ready to wow spectators at classic boat regattas in the Mediterranean!

What tips can you pass to school or university students who would love to work on water?

You spend a lot of your life at work, so it is important to do something you enjoy. If you enjoy your work you are likely to put more into it and be successful as a result, but remember that the marine industry is not as financially rewarding as many other types of work. Be prepared for boring bits with any job, even when it involves sailing! Also, consider that your enjoyment of the sport may be a little diminished when it becomes your work. Immersing yourself in the sport, both during spare time and work time, may be vital to maintain a strong knowledge base and make you effective at the job. ❖

ASSISTANT EDITOR AT MOTOR BOATS MONTHLY – Stewart Campbell

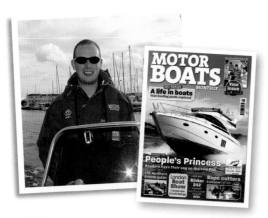

Hi Stewart, can you tell us how you became a journalist on a magazine that specialises in motorboats?

I started my career in newspapers – first in Australia and then China. In 2005 I returned to the UK after a number of years away and was flicking through my dad's copy of Motor Boats Monthly. I was looking for a job and Motor Boats Monthly was looking for a News Editor. It was a match made in heaven.

What does your job at MBM entail?

The work involves a lot of writing, as you'd expect. I'm mainly responsible for the news, many of the features that appear in the magazine and helping the Editor run the good ship MBM.

Is your job exciting and glamorous?

The job certainly has its moments of glamour and excitement, and there's always opportunity to get out on the water. But as a news and features writer primarily, I'm more involved with the issues behind boating. It's the guys who fly all over the world to test boats who you could say have the really glamorous jobs. But then they don't get to pester the RYA for comment about breaking news stories!

What is the best and worst aspect of working as a yachting journalist?

I'm not sure there is a bad aspect to being a boating journalist. If you love the water and boats, then it's the perfect career. Having said that, there are occasions in the depths of winter, when you're out on the water and wish you were behind a desk. But thankfully that doesn't happen too often. The best bits are being able to mess about on boats and meet some incredibly interesting people. Boat owners are a rare breed and you're never far from an interesting story. .

What tips can you give to a young person who would like to pursue a career?

Some of the guys at MBM have no formal journalism training – they just know boats inside and out. So if your knowledge is as encyclopaedic as their's, then you've got a head start. The next thing to do is find a story, write it up and send it to a boating magazine. A lot of magazines rely heavily on freelance contributions and are always on the lookout for exciting new writers. Of course, a formal qualification can't hurt, so have a look at where you can take an NCTJ-accredited journalism course (National Council for the Training of Journalists).

If someone wants to work on water, what alternative career options with motorboats would you recommend?

I've always thought the life of a delivery skipper must be quite interesting: travelling all over the world, new ports every day, helming a huge variety of boats. Otherwise you could sell them, build them, maintain them, or, like me, write about them. The Cowes-based UKSA puts together a free boating careers guide, which is worth a read. ❖

EDITOR AT YACHTING MONTHLY
Paul Gelder

Paul, how did you become editor of a yachting magazine?

Luck and good timing! I was a weekend sailor working as a newspaper editor. At Southampton Boat Show, I was chatting to Yachting Monthly's Features Editor, who told me he was leaving. So I wrote to the editor and got the job. It was like being given a passport to unlimited waterborne adventures. Three months after joining, I sailed with Robin Knox-Johnston from the Azores to Plymouth on his round the world yacht Suhaili. I've been editor since 2002, having worked with, or known, six of the magazine's previous editors.

What does your job entail?

There are nine full-time staff, including the art editor, a staff photographer and three writers. There are also lots of top drawer contributors. I commission articles and oversee the selection of photos and illustrations. The magazine has a great heritage so we have to maintain the highest standards. I start work at 7.30am, on the train to Waterloo, reading proofs and manuscripts. I get home at 7.30pm and often spend a few hours at the weekend catching up on emails and planning features. Other work involves our website, plus publisher and marketing meetings. I have to balance budgets,

recruit and train new staff, and represent the magazine at events.

Is your job rewarding?

I feel immensely privileged. I've been paid to indulge my passion, meet my sailing heroes and go sailing on some extraordinary boats in beautiful places. The high spots are celebrating the magazine's 100th birthday with a centenary issue and our campaign to save Gipsy Moth IV and sail her around the world. I regret not having time for more writing, but see an editor's job as orchestrating and overseeing everyone else's.

What is best and worst about your job?

The best are all the above. Plus never knowing what the next day will bring, and enjoying the buzz of the rush to meet deadlines. The people you meet in the sailing world are a terrific bunch. It seems to be a sport that brings out the best in people. The worst aspect for me is the daily grind of commuting.

What tips can you give to a young person who would like to be a yachting journalist?

Opportunities are rare in such a specialised field. Do your homework. Know your subject, whether the magazine covers ocean racing, round-the-cans racing, or cruising. You need an inquisitive mind and a keen interest in people. Above all, you have to convince editors you're dedicated, passionate and determined. Remember that stories are about people. Good contacts are the key to getting the best stories and the inside track that will make you a successful writer. How to find a job? Keep pestering editors! Apply for Yachting Monthly's bi-annual Geoff Pack Scholarship!

■ **www.yachtingmonthly.co.uk**   ❖

SAILING TV PRODUCER – Digby Fox

Digby was Live Producer of the 2007 America's Cup, Series Producer of Sky's Watersports World and TV producer behind many sailing world championships.

How to get there

Getting any job in TV is tough. Colleges churn out thousands of media graduates all chasing very few openings. In the UK you can count the number of sailing TV producers on one hand.

Prior experience…

Quite a few producers are ex-journalists. I started out as a journalist, getting a Postgrad Diploma, then writing features for Yachts & Yachting and ending up as Editor of Sailing Today. Thirteen years in print taught me about story telling and built up my contacts.

Breaking in…

My break into TV came out of the blue. Andrew Preece, God bless him, recommended me for a job on a match racing production. The company liked what I did and offered me a full time role as a Series Producer for a show on Sky Sports, which I did for six years. All that time in an edit suite taught me how to put TV stories together.

The highs…

It's a wonderful job. I love it. It's creative, dynamic, difficult but immensely rewarding. TV crews get incredible access. I love going to an event, figuring out what's what and who's who, then focusing whatever resources I have on telling the story of the event in moving images. I've had some phenomenal responses to work I've done, and that's cool. The best fun I've had was working as a cameraman on board all the America's Cup boats for the three-year build-up to the 2007 event, and then working as Live Producer for the gig itself.

The lows…

Airports. Check-ins. Planes. Flying.

Making money…

I've been freelance for four years now, and luckily the phone keeps ringing and jobs keep coming up. Like any freelance though, the only security is the contacts you've built up and regular clients – so you have to work on that. I've grown my skills to be able to work as a broadcast cameraman, editor and producer, and all those jobs are paid on a daily rate. I also put budgets and broadcast packages together. Plus I do shows and DVDs on cooking, wine, finance – whatever!

Opportunities…

No jobs will be advertised. Everything is word of mouth/reputation/contacts. TV is reliant on technical skills and a freelance editor can command an excellent daily rate. That would be the route I'd go. Being a cameraman is an amazing job, but I am asked every week by awesomely talented shooters with mainstream credits if there's any work on. To work as a junior assistant or AP (Assistant Producer), you'd have to look at bigger companies. Only one mid-sized outfit, APP (part of Sunset & Vine), specialises in sailing. Otherwise, get onto a sailing magazine and build up your knowledge and contacts through the journalism route.

■ **www.digbyfox.tv**   ❖

SY Antares built by Royal Huisman, in the front line of
superb sailing yachts staffed by a professional crew.

Nitschi/Royal Huisman

SUPERYACHTS & CHARTER YACHTS

16

Working on superyachts is the holy grail of working on water, renowned for fabulous boats, celebrity guests, a billionaire lifestyle and great earnings for the crew. But is the superyacht and charter scene as great as it's made out to be? What is the good, the bad and the ugly? To find out, we asked a superyacht careers specialist and got viewpoints from three different crew...

ASKJOEY – Joey Meen

Joey Meen is a consultant who specialises in superyacht crew careers and training.

Joey, how did you begin working in the superyacht industry?

This is the 17th year I have been involved with superyacht crew and their training. I was introduced to the superyacht industry through Plymouth Sailing School, which I ran for ten years. The RYA required the Yachtmaster Offshore qualification to be taken in tidal waters and I had a constant stream of crew flying to the UK from all over the world to complete RYA Yachtmaster courses. Then I moved to France in 2002 to help run the training department at Freedom Yachting with Steve Emerson. (Steve was sadly terminally ill at the time and died soon after my arrival. Steve was the founder of Freedom Yachting and previous Principal of Plymouth Sailing School.)

Over the years I have developed an in-depth knowledge of the training and certification regulation systems of both the RYA and MCA. I am well trusted by both associations to ensure that standards are upheld. I also represent the crews as honorary secretary for the Professional Yachtsmen's Association.

The PYA (www.pya.org) are the only association who work hard primarily for the benefit of all crew, in all disciplines. They have members from 45 countries and representatives worldwide. The PYA is consulted on and influences changes in laws and regulations for the yachting industry.

What service does Askjoey provide?

Askjoey is the first stop for anyone considering training for a career in yachting and those moving up the qualification ladder. I deal with a continuous stream of yachtsmen and women who are baffled by the regulations, unsure of what training they need, how to apply for an NOE (Notice of Eligibility), fill out training records and generally plan their large training investment. They really need and appreciate honest, unbiased (reasonably priced) advice and help with checking and processing their documents. I am also very aware that their confusion creates a huge workload for the MCA (Maritime & Coastguard Agency) as well as training providers, dealing with processes and questions that I can more easily help with. I offer career advice as well as help with MCA training record books, international certification, training compatibility, training programmes and attesting documents.

Is superyacht work mainly seasonal or available year-round?

There are a variety of employment options, from full time to seasonal, private yachts and charter. A busy charter boat has the potential for crew to be working very long hours for three or more months continuously, so burnout is inevitable. The industry does tend to be seasonal, which means crew can take advantage of the benefits of good salaries with tips and time-off between seasons.

The 174 foot alloy ketch Salperton caters for up to ten guests, served by crew living in six ensuite cabins. Facilities include a fully fitted gym.

Navico

If crew want a more 'stable' lifestyle, then a full time position on a private or less busy charter boat might suit them better, but of course the income would be relative. Even so, summer and winter seasons are always busy, with little or no time off.

What are conditions generally like for crew?

Crew generally have good living conditions, particularly if you compare them to other types of commercial shipping. Most boats have communal living areas for the crew. Cabins are usually shared and can be quite small, but are usually plush with good facilities. Some of the larger boats have extra facilities for crew including WiFi, Satellite TV, crew chefs and perhaps access to the onboard gym. This does not always apply! Space is always limited on any boat, but crew should have enough space in their cabin for selected personal items.

The MCA have confirmed that the UK Government is committed to ratification of the MLC (Maritime Labour Convention) by 2010. This involves developing legislative proposals to align existing UK law and practice with the new convention and planning the introduction of a new inspection and certification regime for UK ships. Part of this convention includes a new standard to yacht builds, which will implement minimum cabin size and crew space per person.

Do charter clients or owners treat their crew with respect?

The types of people who own boats or can afford to charter them are used to, and expect, an extremely high standard in every discipline of their lives. On the whole, owners and charter guests treat crew very well, but like any hospitality industry there is always someone who has a fly in their soup! With private boats, the seasoned owners are usually fully aware that it is in their interest to keep crew happy. They have to be able to trust crew, so they generally take measures to have a good rapport and keep them for as long as possible, sometimes offering incentives like paying for courses or pension schemes. But you still may encounter the odd difficult owner! The main complaints by crew about bad treatment from guests usually concern short-term charter clients. Sadly, some guests rock up with an attitude that is disrespectful to the boat and consequently disrespectful to the crew.

> **I deal with a continuous stream of yachtsmen and women who are baffled by the regulations, unsure of what training they need...**

Do you get friction between crew? For instance, are some skippers difficult to work for?

Crew live, work, breathe and eat together – of course there are times of tension. It's up to the captain and officers to learn intelligent people skills and keep the crew happy and working as a team. Every captain will have a horror story to tell and two of the biggest attributes for working in this industry are tolerance and patience. You have to be a team player – or don't sign up!

What qualifications and experience are necessary to work on a superyacht at ground level? Is it possible to start with no qualifications at all? Is it a big advantage to invest a lot of money in superyacht courses run by 'zero to hero' organisations?

Gone are the days of backpackers rocking up for a few months' work, mainly due to popular demand that all crew should hold the STCW95 crew safety-training modules (consisting of basic training in Fire Fighting, Sea Survival, First Aid, Personal Safety and Social Responsibilities).

Large or small? Working on a 100 foot plus yacht is very different from skippering a cruiser, with the focus of hospitality and maximum guest satisfaction.

These courses are imperative for individual safety, not to mention the safety of your fellow crew and the vessel. Most crew that come into the superyacht industry are looking for a career. Whether it's a short term or long term career, some financial investment on training is unavoidable. But I never encourage a large financial investment, unless the crew member is absolutely sure they want to embark on yachting as a career, which means they should have at least one season under their belt. Also, I would always encourage getting the personal medical completed first (ENG1 or equivalent). It's too late to discover you are colour blind or suffer from diabetes when you have already spent the money on your courses.

Sadly, training providers that offer fast track courses have got a bad reputation in the

superyacht community. This is not necessarily due to the level or duration of the course – it's more because crew sometimes arrive with inflated expectations beyond merit. However, it seems that these training facilities no longer encourage crew to expect high-ranking positions, just because they have a qualification. They are also being encouraged to spread the courses out over three or more years. It is worth mentioning that the MCA have designed a stepping-stone of courses and modules that are specific to the yachting industry. They will not allow someone to use those qualifications to cross over to any other type of commercial shipping, whereas it can be possible to cross over to yachting from a merchant or commercial education. None of this can be done in a rush.

...continued over...

Ready for the guests. Sailing Yacht William Tai (ex Surama).

Roy Roberts/Royal Huisman

up to the individual crew member to arrange payment of personal taxes, but the boat will usually arrange visas if required.

Do boys and girls get equal opportunities when applying for work on superyachts?

On the whole, I think boys and girls get a fair look-in, with more and more girls joining the deck and engineering. I know many captains who like to have a balance of girls and boys in each department. This has certainly become a trend in the last few years, but sadly the odd 'old fashioned' captains can be prejudiced towards female deckies or engineers. It's not always the captain who chooses crew, particularly on private boats, when it's really up to the owner to say what crew they want to live with. I guess it's similar to hiring domestic help in your home! One thing to bear in mind is that boy/girl cabin shares and availability may also determine the make-up of the crew.

As a very rough example, it would take a minimum of 6 years with an outlay of approx £20,000 in training fees to reach a Master 3000gt, which is the highest yacht qualification.

Above all, this is a very small industry. To get to and stay at the top and have a valued reputation can only be achieved from hard work and experience, which includes longevity, loyalty, discretion, trustworthiness, subservience, tolerance, patience and above all respect.

How much can you earn? How do crew manage visas or taxes?

There is no overall 'wage guide'. Some crew agencies use an in-house guide, but even that varies from agent to agent. Potential income will depend on position, experience, size of vessel and the itinerary. There is also a difference between charter and private yacht salaries. It is

What are the best aspects of working on superyachts? What are the worst aspects?

It seems that by its very definition, working on a superyacht has been glamorised. Being in the proximity of the rich and famous on floating 5 star hotels has many perks, ranging from travel to an education in fine foods and wines, which are all part of a luxury lifestyle. But the bottom line is anyone working in the hospitality industry has a subservient role, throughout the ranks, and it's a hard-working industry. I would say you have to be a certain type of person with particular attributes – not dissimilar to those who become teachers or nurses – to come into this non-conventional industry.

What advice would you give to a young person, fresh out of school or university, who would like to work on a superyacht?

There is a career ladder in all disciplines, which offers the chance of a profession. Many school leavers who don't have the desire to go onto further education would find this an interesting balance. It's good to have some background in the discipline you want to get into. For example, if you were looking at the deck side, a background in varnishing or sanding would be useful. For those looking at working in the interior, bar work, table service or a cleaning background would be good. Quite often the head of the interior department comes from butler school or a similar hotelier background. If you are looking at working in the engineering department, then it would be good to have some kind of apprentice or work experience with mechanical or electrical engineering. Or maybe you are looking at becoming a chef, in which case you would need to have completed some formal training to start as a second or crew chef.

How do you find a yacht to work on?

You need to put a relevant CV together and then visit the numerous crew agencies. It's all about being available immediately for interview, being prepared and able to travel and being smart and well groomed at a moment's notice. It is essential that you present yourself at an interview as someone who would fit into a 5 star environment and is serious enough to offer the expected extremely high standards of service – deck, engineer and interior alike!

The best time of year to look for work is from March to April, when boats are looking for their summer crew. The European season usually runs from May to September, or earlier depending on the Easter break. Start looking for work in the Caribbean from September, ready for the season from November to February.

■ askjoey@wanadoo.fr   ❖

> **I know many captains who like to have a balance of girls and boys in each department... but the odd 'old fashioned' captains can be prejudiced towards female deckies or engineers.**

WORKING ON SUPERYACHTS

The Good: The amazing and interesting people you meet, the countries you visit, the lifestyle you dip in and out of... not to mention the salary. It's a wonderful career for the right person – you can quickly get hooked.

The Bad & the Ugly: Not seeing your family for months, transient friendships, watching countries whiz past through the porthole, not stepping off the boat for months on end, living with the same people day in and day out with minimal personal space.

The Overview: It's about being the professional and having a smile on your face every day. It's about taking a pride in what you do. It's about integrity, performance and attention to detail. Everything must shine, including you! It takes a unique kind of person who can keep their cool with the day-to-day demands of working in the superyacht industry.

12 MONTHS IN THE LIFE OF A BOAT WORKER – Jonathan Medway

Jonathan and his father Robert on board Altair

In the early autumn of 2007, nineteen year old Jonathan Medway helped deliver a Beneteau First 40.7 charter boat from the south of England to the Canary Islands. He had intended to fly home to England, but spotted an advert on the wall of a dockside bar in Las Palmas, posted by an owner who needed more crew for his Swan 48 in the ARC racing class. Jonathan signed on, all expenses paid, to race the Swan across the Atlantic to St Lucia, where he then spent two more weeks preparing the yacht for a Caribbean season.

"Remember that a yacht is a working environment and respect other people's space!"

After cruising down to Bequia with friends, Jonathan took a local flight to Antigua in late December in order to look for work. He tried a crew agency, but they said he hadn't a hope without any formal sailing qualifications such as STCW and RYA Yachtmaster, despite having many years of sailing experience. So Jonathan walked round the dock and talked to as many people as possible in English Harbour, eventually landing his first job as a 'day worker' by the end of January.

Having worked as a house painter and decorator in the UK, Jonathan was well qualified to varnish the enormous wooden spars of the classic schooner Altair, one of the great designs by William Fife. In fact there was so much day work to be done that Jonathan was soon on Altair every day, which led to the opportunity to crew during the St Barts Bucket regatta in February. At that stage Jonathan wasn't paid to go sailing, but like all the crew was put up in a superb hotel and enjoyed a lot of good food.

Getting paid to sail...

As time went on, Jonathan began to get paid to sail, though he says "...not much". This was partly thanks to a high turnover of crew on board Altair, with some appearing to lack useful experience despite their apparent high qualifications. Jonathan raced on Altair during Antigua Race Week, then helped sail her across the Atlantic with a delivery crew, stopping at the Azores and sheltering in southern Ireland due to very rough weather, before heading to the Clyde in Scotland for the Fife Regatta of classic yachts.

He continued to live and work on board Altair until the end of the European sailing season, but like most of the crew was never given a contract, so was aware there was no security. After racing at the Pendennis Cup regatta in Falmouth, he insisted on taking a week's holiday to sail with friends at the Cowes Classic Regatta, then rejoined Altair on passage to the

Altair lies alongside at Falmouth, before heading for Ibiza and St Tropez.

Mediterranean, visiting Ibiza before racing at the Royale Regate de Cannes and Voiles de St Tropez. It was the culmination of working on one of the world's finest classic yachts, but Jonathan had decided it was also time to move on for a number of reasons. Altair was a physically tough boat to sail and they were often short-handed. He also got fed up with living on top of people in a confined space and all the crew found it difficult to live up to the exacting standards of the skipper, who consequently had a rapid turnover in crew. Working on Altair had also effectively become 24/7, with endless sanding, varnishing and general maintenance, none of which are as much fun as racing!

Would he do it again?

Sailing on Altair was a wonderful experience and Jonathan had also saved quite a lot of money, with no expenses and all payment offshore without tax. If the right job came along,

he would go back to working on deck, but cautions that racing crew normally don't get paid well unless they are very well established, so it's better to be fully employed with more mundane work.

For those who want to follow suit, Antigua is the place to be in December or January, after which the scene shifts to Palma, Antibes or Cannes in April. Jonathan found that you don't necessarily need STCW or Yachtmaster qualifications to work on a private yacht, but you do to work on a charter yacht as they are required for insurance. As time goes on, he predicts that qualifications will become more and more essential and it may be difficult to find work without them.

Finally, if you get the opportunity to pick and choose which boat you work on, Jonathan's advice is, "Working with people you can get on with is a lot more important than working on the world's most wonderful boat!" ❖

WORKING AS A DECKHAND – Max Abbott

Max, how did you start working on a superyacht?

I received a call from my good friend Tom Miller, who offered me some day work on the yacht Parsifal III at La Spezia in Northern Italy, lasting two weeks. At that time I was part way through a course in outdoor education in Bristol and those two weeks would have paid for two months rent, so I jumped at the opportunity. However, when the skipper offered me a longer job after the first week, I ditched my course and joined the crew!

Have you found work on other yachts?

I only worked on Parsifal III, before deciding it was time to study for a degree. But the same friend who got me started is now skipper of a lovely Royal Huisman 95 foot ketch based in La Ciotat. I don't actively seek work on yachts, but if he gives me a call I will always go and help – jobs for the boys and all that!

What is your experience of a typical working day for a deckhand?

On charter, rise at 5am, wash and shammy the whole boat. Make sure all towels and other bits are ready for the guests. Weigh anchor, sails up, sails down, sails up again, sails down again, drop anchor, tenders in water, toys in water, toys out, tenders out, toys in, tenders in, shore-run with guests, toys out again and again and again. During the evening, help with serving dinners and do more shore-runs for the guests, which may run as late as 5am. Anchor watch through the night. Not much really…

Off charter, varnish capping rails, acid on the decks to make them shine, clean and polish topsides. Fix, repair, paint, antifoul and clean the bilges. In fact, the list is endless. Basically start on the bow, work to the stern, and then do it all over again.

What is the best part of working on a superyacht? What is the worst part?

You can travel the world, see amazing places, meet amazing people and get lots of money. But it's not so nice dealing with the drug culture, sailing through hurricanes and having stuff break on charters. Also beware of psychotic captains and guests who have lost their grip on reality.

Did you have to sign a contract that locks you into working for a specific length of time?

I never signed a contract in one year on board Parsifal III.

What was the money like?

The pay was the main reason I did it, although the tips were better. Sometimes I was tipped the equivalent of a month's wages for one week on charter.

What were conditions like for the crew?

We were fed well and had plenty of room, with a bunk each. Conditions were generally very good, although verbals from the skipper were a little hard to handle when he was on one of his episodes.

Did owners and charterers always treat the crew with respect?

The owner always treated me very fairly when he was on board. When he was off the boat, it was a little more difficult as he had no concept of how difficult it was to get things done in real time. Charter guests were generally very kind and polite, if not a little demanding at times.

Was there ever friction between the crew?

There was some tension with our chef. He was a great person, but had a fierce temper! Most arguments were trivial and blew over. Living on a yacht is too closed an environment to hold on to tension or be bitchy in any way.

What advice would you give to a young person, fresh out of school or university, who would like to work on a superyacht?

Do your STCW95, then fly somewhere like Antibes, Monaco or St Maarten and sign up with an agency. Always be a 'yes' man. If that fails, walk the dock and ask every single person you see – a business card with your picture and phone number helps. And have a CV ready wherever you are at whatever time of day.

What experience and skills are required?

I went in green, but the market is now being flooded by guys with STCW95. If you are keen and willing to learn and can prove yourself to an understanding skipper, you should get a foot in the door – the yachting industry is still quite 'old school' in this way. Knowing how to sail, having good personal skills and always giving it your best are a must.

Max takes a stroll on Parsifal III.

As far as I am aware, STCW is mandatory on all MCA registered yachts operating in the open seas. First Mate must hold 'Officer of the Watch'. Depending on the tonnage and waterline, skipper must hold Yachtmaster Ocean and relevant Captain's first aid up to a class 4/3.

Do boys and girls get equal opportunities when applying for work on yachts?

Usually boys on deck and girls in the saloon. Equal opportunities don't seem to apply at sea, but I think it's changing slowly.

Would you recommend working on superyachts as a short term or long term career?

That depends. If you know you want to have the stress of skippering a very expensive boat until you're 40, and then have a nervous breakdown after missing your kids grow up and watching your wife leave because you're never there, then I would say a long-term career is OK. But if you want to earn a fast buck and have a good time, then make it short term.

Anything you would like to add?

I had the time of my life on Parsifal III. If I had no commitments in the UK, I would have another crack at it for sure. ❖

RUNNING A CHARTER YACHT
Gordon Young and Clare Marriage

Gordon Young and Clare Marriage manage a 72 foot performance cruising sloop based in the Mediterranean. Gordon works as captain, while Claire works as as mate, chef and hostess…

THE CAPTAIN

Hi Gordon, can you explain how you run a 72 foot yacht?

As Captain, I am basically responsible for everything that happens on board, from sailing and navigating to maintenance and presentation. Working on a private yacht is all about image. The yacht has to look its best at all times, even when not on charter. Stainless steel, windows and hull have to be polished and the boat kept clean and tidy all the time. I also have to maintain the various equipment on board, such as winches, blocks, main engine, generator, water maker, hydraulics, electrics, electronics, air conditioning and refrigeration. It sounds daunting, but all the equipment has a manual and the manufacturers are generally very helpful when you phone for advice. Almost all my time when off charter is taken up by maintenance.

There is also correspondence between myself and the owners, the charter brokers and potential or booked charter guests to get on with as well.

When on charter, I usually have a plan of where we will go for the week, but that usually changes due to weather or something different that the guests want to do. I try to do a lot of homework, finding out about 'sights worth seeing' and other useless bits of information. It's all about keeping the guests occupied during the day, since you are pretty much a tour guide as well as a captain!

Once we have stopped for lunch, usually at anchor, I help the chef/hostess with laying the table and serving drinks. Same goes for the evening, when I also help with the washing up – not my favourite job! The evening is when I check to make sure batteries are OK for the night, there is enough fuel in the correct tank and that fresh water and waste levels are all OK. After the guests have finally gone to bed, I do a quick tidy-up and make sure the boat is secure before I get my head down – you definitely learn to sleep with one ear/eye open while at anchor! Then up again at 7am to chamois the boat, making sure it's all clean and tidy before the guests appear. I usually have to do a bread and pastry run for their breakfast as well.

How did your yachting career develop?

My first job after getting my Yachtmaster certificates was as voluntary delivery crew in Australia, where I was based, on 36-60 foot racing yachts. This led to paid delivery jobs, and eventually to working part-time looking after a 38 foot racing yacht. I then did some corporate charter work in Sydney Harbour before heading to Greece to do the obligatory flotilla season.

Working on a private yacht is all about image. The yacht has to look its best at all times, even when not on charter.

After a few months of job searching and doing odd days of work on boats in Scotland, I got a job as lead deck hand on a 40 metre yacht. This was a big step up in terms of complexity and the amount of work I was expected to do. With a crew of eight and myself in charge of sailing, we took the boat across the Pacific. After the boat was sold, I took a few months off, updated some courses and started work with my girlfriend Clare on a 55 foot charter yacht in the South of France. Unfortunately, we didn't get on with the owners (neither did four other sets of crew), so we parted company and now run a 72 foot yacht that is used both for private and charter all over the world.

Has work always been easy to find? Is the work seasonal, or available year-round?

Work seems to be easy to find when you have a job, but harder when you don't! Obviously flotillas are seasonal, but once the Med summer season finishes the Caribbean season is starting. Most of the good jobs are got through word of mouth, so you need to be in the areas where yachts are based – Antibes, Palma, Antigua – to meet people and 'dockwalk'. Having a well presented CV helps a lot.

What is the best part of working on a charter yacht? What is the worst part? Or is it all just fun?

Not all fun! Drifting in a busy shipping lane near Croatia with an engine that has a blocked fuel line, or being in the middle of the Pacific with a generator fire, are two not particularly fun moments from my career! Being on charter, the best part is when you have a great day sailing and the guests are happy, as that means no hassle. The worst is being on call 24 hours a day for every day of the charter.

You get very very tired, but of course you can't show it! When off charter it is great as you can relax and even have weekends off in beautiful locations.

Can you make a good income? Are there hassles with tax or requirements for working in different countries?

The money when you start can be very little – sometimes just your flights and food. Flotilla work is also not very well paid at about 100-150 Euros a week. But as you progress to bigger boats, the pay increases substantially. As an idea, I was earning £1,800 a month on the 40 metre ketch. On the 72 footer, we are just back from a ski holiday that was paid entirely from one tip during the summer! Tax is something we're trying to find out more about. We have not earned anything in the UK and keep the money in an offshore account and separate Euro account. There are no real hassles working in other countries, so long as you have a UK passport and clean criminal record. Most boats will sort out any relevant visas, although the American B1-B2 visa (to work on a non-American boat in American waters) requires a visit to an embassy.

Do charter clients always treat their crew with respect? Do you ever get serious problems?

Thankfully all our guests have been lovely. They expect a lot, as they are paying roughly 24,000 Euros per week, so as long as you can meet those expectations they are happy. Problems have been caused when the charter brokers have sold something that is quite difficult to achieve. For instance, during one 10 day trip we were supposed to cruise around the main ports in the South of France – St Tropez, Cannes and Antibes – then head across to Corsica. This was a 100 nautical mile passage across open sea, with guests who didn't like any waves at all! So it was not really practical or enjoyable. We have heard a few horror stories on the grapevine, but maybe the stories get larger in the telling!

What qualifications and experience do you need for your kind of work?

To work as a Skipper/Captain on a yacht, you will need a Yachtmaster Offshore commercially endorsed certificate. This is also becoming the minimum for deckhands on large yachts, as competition for places allows captains to choose better qualified crew. STCWs are the next minimum qualification for any crew. This is a week long safety course, including personal survival techniques, fire fighting and fire prevention, elementary first aid, personal safety and social responsibility. The courses are a lot of fun and not too hard, but very expensive. When I got my current job, I also had updated my licence to MCA Master 200 (5 week theory course) and done a 1 week engine maintenance course, as well as logging 34,000 nautical miles of sailing experience.

What advice would you give to a younger person who would like to work on a large yacht?

Just get out and do it. Get as much experience in as many different boats and areas as possible. Get your tickets (career development loans can help) and go where the yachts are. Don't be put off if you cannot find something right away.

> **…the best part is when you have a great day sailing and the guests are happy, as that means no hassle. The worst is being on call 24 hours a day for every day of the charter.**

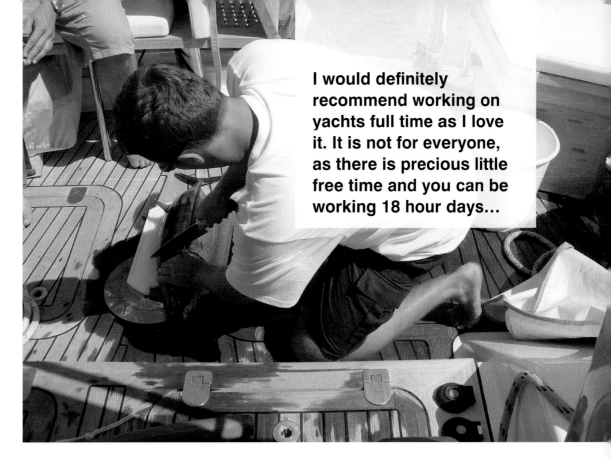

I would definitely recommend working on yachts full time as I love it. It is not for everyone, as there is precious little free time and you can be working 18 hour days...

Are there equal opportunities for boys and girls?

Unfortunately not many mates or captains on larger yachts are female. Although there are a lot of girls in the industry, the norm is that the guy is captain and the girl is the chef/hostess. But quite a few flotilla skippers are female!

Would you recommend working on yachts as a full time career?

I would definitely recommend working on yachts full time as I love it. It is not for everyone, as there is precious little free time and you can be working 18 hour days while on charter (sometimes more) and may have to work very, very hard. But you get to see some of the world's most beautiful places, among which the Galapagos, Tahiti and Croatia are my favourites so far. I get to go sailing a lot and enjoy the technical challenge of looking after such a complicated boat. Also no day is the same so there is little chance of getting bored.

The money is also very good and you should be able to save a large amount if you are sensible. I have a friend who has just bought a property with no mortgage, all thanks to savings from working on yachts.

THE MATE

Clare, how did you and Gordon get to run a yacht as a couple?

My partner had already been working on yachts for a few years before I joined him, so this helped our joint effort to find work together. Finding work as a couple can be very hard work when you start, so you need to be prepared to be patient. Often, crew agencies will suggest that you split up for the first year or two and hope that a suitable vacancy will come up on one or the other's yacht. Once you both have experience, it's a lot easier to market yourselves as a 'couple' .

We were very lucky to be offered a job running a charter yacht. Having signed up for every possible crew agency and crew job website, to ensure our CVs were available to as many employers as possible, we then got our first job from a website which we thought would be of no use whatsoever! Once we were employed, we still made sure we kept up-to-date with the crew agencies and websites, just in case we needed to start looking again and also because our first contract was only for one season. We always made sure we made as many contacts as possible within the industry.

In general terms, how easy is it to find good jobs on yachts? Is most work seasonal or full time?

Within the yacht industry, many of the jobs available are only publicised through word of mouth. It can be a very tough industry to find work, especially at the beginning because there are now so many qualifications available. It's become hard to get in as a Yachtmaster, because you're up against people with many more qualifications. A big problem is that yachts are generally not keen on hiring inexperienced crew, even if they do have the correct qualifications, but you can't get any experience without being offered a job! Once you have the experience and the all-important contacts, it makes finding work a lot easier. There are lots of vacancies on yachts that need filling, but unfortunately employers can be picky because so many people apply for each position.

The work can be both seasonal or year-round, with charter and flotilla companies tending to hire seasonal staff only. This usually means being based in the Med during the summer and the Caribbean during the winter. If you are attracted to privately owned yachts, which may charter as well, the work is more likely to be longer term with a permanent contract.

What are the best and worst aspects of working on a charter yacht?

The best part is being able to see all these incredible places in the world, some of which are only accessible by boat, and to experiment with all the wonderful fresh produce available around the world. It's also such a compliment to see your guests enjoying themselves and how grateful they are for all your effort and hard work. Being a chef on board can be one of the most rewarding (as well as most difficult!) positions. You may think that the guests are most interested in being on a yacht, but it's the food that really counts! At the end of a hard day's work, it's the most amazing feeling when the guests start gushing about how wonderful all the meals have been and asking how on earth you can produce such wonders in such a small galley. The worst part is the long days and long hours you need to work. It's all hugely rewarding, but can be very draining without much time to yourself whilst you have guests on board. You also need to be prepared to make sacrifices, by being away from your family and friends for long periods of time.

> **Being a chef on board can be one of the most rewarding positions. You may think that the guests are most interested in being on a yacht, but it's the food that really counts!**

Can you make a good income? How do you handle bureaucracy?

Your income depends on your position and level of experience, but generally it's a very nice money earner. As a chef, your level of experience really makes a difference. The chef's position is very high paying if you are able to climb up the ranks to a superyacht.

One of the main bonuses of working on yachts is that you are officially living 'offshore' which makes you exempt from tax as long as you spend a certain number of months away from home. It can be a complex process to become fully exempt but is well worth it. You also don't have the usual daily expenses that most people onshore need to pay. All food onboard is included, with no rent, gas or electricity bills. Much of your income can be saved and put away every month, apart from some beer money!

There are requirements for working in certain countries. Jobs advertised often ask for crew with the B1/B2 visa if the yacht is a frequent visitor to US waters, but it's fairly hard to get the visa unless you are employed. You will also need a visa to work in Australian waters, although their rules have recently been relaxed and make it much easier for larger yachts to visit.

How do you secure charter clients?

Our yacht has a main charter broker based in France to manage our clients. It is up to them to market the yacht to fellow brokers around the world. Crew are often encouraged to help brokers by marketing the yacht themselves, and if successful are rewarded with a bonus (a cut of the charter price).

Do clients always treat their crew with respect?

Some guests can be very difficult and demanding, yet others can be an absolute delight to have onboard. The key is to be strong and not let any moaning guests get in the way of doing the best possible job. It's so important to listen to their moans and keep them as happy as possible, because they are usually paying a huge amount of money to charter the yacht and will expect the very best. It's vital to remember that each guest will want different things, so make sure you communicate as much as possible to gauge what they want out of their

time onboard, especially when it comes to food preferences. Often, they will have filled out a preference sheet with all their likes, dislikes and dietary requirements, but it's always useful to ask again once they come onboard. All requests need to be considered and every effort made to try to fulfil them within reason. If the safety of a crew member or the yacht is at risk, then a line needs to be drawn.

More serious problems are possible, since yachts are susceptible to all sorts of mechanical failure. We once had to end our charter two days early because of a breakdown. We were lucky because the guests were very understanding, after realising there was nothing we could have done to prevent this from happening. If there is a problem, it's important to make sure everything else is spot on. This usually means the chef is on over-drive and lobster comes out for dinner! But anything can go wrong. For instance, you should always have a back up plan in case there's a major problem in the galley. This might create a long pause between courses, in which case it's always good to tell your guests there may be a small wait rather than leave them twiddling their thumbs. They will be happier in the long run.

What qualifications and experience do you need for your kind of work?

To work as a chef, most yachts will require you to have STCW95. If it's a smaller sailing yacht, they may also like you to have some sailing qualifications, so you can help out on deck when not in the galley. For chef qualifications, most will look for some formal training, with many of the larger superyachts only employing chefs with experience in restaurants or on similar yachts. On the smaller yachts, experience as a chef may not be necessary, so long as you have had some formal training. A one-day food hygiene course is a must, but this is often included in many cookery courses that are available. Some cookery courses are tailored towards working on yachts and will usually last a month – check out the Rosie Davies cookery school near Bath at www.rosiedavies.co.uk. Other courses may require a year-long diploma.

> It's so important to listen to their moans and keep them as happy as possible, because they are usually paying a huge amount of money to charter the yacht…

What advice would you give to someone who would like to work on large yachts?

I would suggest keeping a level head. Often you come across fresh-faced Yachtmasters who expect to find a job straight away, but this won't happen unless you are very lucky. It's important to be patient and make sure you spend time making contacts with crew agencies and other crew members – find out their local hang-outs and talk to people, but don't start harassing them for jobs or they will walk away. Just be there to make friends.

Another good way of getting yourself seen and heard is to do some dock walking. You will need to be at the dock at 7am, smartly dressed and ready to work, doing anything from scrubbing the decks to polishing. It can be really dull, but the more effort you put in, the more likely the crew will take some notice of you. Never walk onto a yacht if you can't find someone to ask you up on deck – just come back later on. It really is a case of starting from the bottom and working your way up, however qualified you think you may be. If you haven't got much experience, they will expect you to start from scratch.

Loosely speaking, a yacht will have female interior crew and male deck crew, although there is certainly not a firm line between the two. There are many successful female captains and mates/deckhands and lots of male chefs and stewards. It can often come down to the sleeping arrangements as to which sex they are looking for when filling a position. However, working on yachts can be a very sexist industry. A male, purely due to his greater strength or the sleeping arrangements, may beat a female applying for a deckhand position.

Would you recommend working on yachts as a full time career?

It really depends on the individual. One advantage of the industry is that once you are more experienced and further up the ladder, you may be able to work on a rotational basis, normally working three months on the yacht and then having three months paid holiday. This is a huge benefit if you want to start a family or wish to have a base on land for a few months of the year. One other advantage of the industry is that you gain so many good skills that can be transferred to a land based job. There are also lots of land based yachting jobs available, so you may not need to leave the industry at all!

■ **www.gordonandclare.com**   ❖

WORKING ON YACHTS

Yachts of less than 24 metres (78 feet LOA)

■ **Essential requirements for the crew:** Although no formal qualifications may be required, many skippers will prefer to take crew who have undergone training to at least Day Skipper level. If you look for work through a crew placement agency, they will often recommend that you hold a Day Skipper certificate, supported by training such as the Diesel Engine and Radar courses.

■ **Essential requirements for the skipper:** Necessary qualifications are determined by the area in which the yacht is operating. With the Coastal Skipper certificate of competence you can skipper yachts of up to 24 metres, operating up to 20 miles from a safe haven. The Yachtmaster Offshore certificate of competence enables you to skipper yachts up to 200GT (gross tonnage), 150 miles from a safe haven. The Yachtmaster Ocean certificate of competence enables you to work worldwide. All of these certificates must be commercially endorsed.

Yachts over 24 metres (78 feet LOA) and up to 200GT (gross tonnage)

■ **Essential requirements for the crew:** You may need an MCA Yacht Rating Certificate as a certain number of crew on board are required to be qualified. For this you should hold RYA Day Skipper or Watch Leader and Competent Crew certificates and will need additional STCW training in sea survival, fire fighting and prevention, first aid, personal safety and social responsibilities. In addition to the skipper, a typical superyacht crew may include a first mate, engineer, bosun, hostess, chef and deck crew.

■ **Essential requirements for the skipper:** Any skipper of a British flagged private or commercial yacht of this size, operating in UK and many non-UK ports, must hold an RYA Yachtmaster Offshore or Ocean Certificate of Competence with commercial endorsement. To enable your qualifications to be valid worldwide and on non-British yachts, you can take three short MCA courses on fire fighting, first aid and social responsibilities to obtain the STCW endorsement on your RYA certificate of competence.

Bareboat Skipper

■ The duties of a bareboat skipper include the preparation of yachts for charter and their delivery, as well as acting as skipper on a charter. On a small yacht, the bareboat skipper will have to live with the charterers, possibly for as long as two weeks. In addition to failsafe yacht handling skills, refined social skills may be required. The usual minimum requirement for bareboat skippers is a commercially endorsed RYA Yachtmaster Offshore Certificate of Competence.

*Painstaking restoration of the yacht Lucky Girl
by a craftsman at Fairlie Restorations.*

CLASSIC YACHT RESTORATION & REPLICAS

17

Restorations, classic yacht replicas and traditionally built new yachts can provide a wonderful opportunity to create waterborne works of art. Fairlie Restorations is not only dedicated to preserving the work of the great classic yacht designer William Fife, but also designs and builds its own modern classics for the most discerning and wealthy owners.

ANCIENT OR MODERN?

Duncan Walker runs Fairlie Restorations, one of the world's leading yards specialising in restoring and building replicas of classic yachts.

Duncan, could you tell us what you do at Fairlie Restorations?

FR was set up in 1990 to restore classic yachts, specifically those built by William Fife. We own his design archive of 600 yachts from 1884 to 1944 and hence can build replicas. We have built two new yachts, the last one designed in house by our naval architect Paul Spooner. This last yacht is our future direction, designed as a traditional long keel sailing boat, but built using modern timber technology and with 21st century deck gear and rig including carbon fibre spars, boom roller reefing mainsail and roller reefing headsails.

How did you get into this kind of work?

My family lived in NW London and I discovered my interest in things nautical when my father built five small boats, plus an uncle founded Sea Ventures, the first bareboat yacht charter company in the UK. I developed a love of sailing in my teenage years, then on to university to study production engineering and management. After an unfulfilling time in engineering, I ran away to sea at the age of 28 and spent five years as a professional yachtsman. I became part of the commissioning crew of the famous schooner Jessica, joined the Altair restoration project, rebuilt Maiden, started work on the classic Fife yacht Tuiga and set up Fairlie in 1989.

Fairlie Restorations

Fine detail work on the 18 metre cruising yacht Niebla, designed by Paul Spooner and newly built by Fairlie Restorations as a modern classic for limited production.

How many people do you employ? What qualifications or experience do they require?

We employ two designers, one a fully qualified Naval Architect, plus approximately sixteen wood workers, split 50/50 between traditional shipwrights and bench joiners. The majority are time served apprentices, all with Level 2 City & Guilds boatbuilding qualifications, varying in age from 62 to 18. The number of tradesmen with experience in traditional yacht building is rapidly decreasing, which is why we try to take an apprentice every year.

Is yacht restoration rewarding in terms of personal satisfaction or making money?

No one should go into boatbuilding for the money, only the satisfaction of building beautiful things!

"One of the biggest challenges is finding and developing the key tradesmen who are enthused to work in our unique sector – and get paid as well!"

Mariquita is the largest Fairlie restoration project, rescued and salvaged from a mud berth. She is the only surviving example of the 19 metre IRC class.

Fairlie Restorations

Only the super-rich can support this level of craftsmanship.

Does the future look good for yacht restoration and replica building?

It is very difficult to smooth out the cyclical nature of our business, which is either feast or famine. We are running short of restoration projects, since there is a diminishing supply of classic yachts, so the future is undoubtedly in new vessels, whether replicas or designed in-house.

Would you recommend it as a career?

Selfishly yes, since we need people to train up in traditional boatbuilding techniques to keep those skills alive. But don't expect to get rich.

What advice would you give to a young person at school or university, or someone looking for a career change, who would like to get into yacht restoration?

A university degree is not a lot of good. A high degree of manual skill is required plus experience in woodwork, augmented by specialist training courses. The ideal age to start is 18, when we can provide training through day release in City & Guilds boatbuilding and Level 3 NVQs with a recognised training provider.

■ www.fairlierestorations.com   ❖

"I'VE HAD ENOUGH!"

Peter Lacey realised he was steadily going nuts, when a voice in his head cried, "I've had enough!" After 40 years of working as aa tax consultant, he woke up one morning, ready for the daily commute to London, returning home exhausted at 8pm. So Peter decided to change from earning lots of money with very little enjoyable time, to earning very little money with lots of enjoyable time.

Peter had amassed a small collection of traditional wooden sailing dinghies, a magnificent 38 foot wooden motor yacht built in the 1950s and classic cars including a Jaguar XK120, all of which needed extensive restoration. The hassle and expense of getting other people to do this work sent Peter in a new direction. He had always enjoyed working with his hands, so it was a toss-up between signing on for a course in boat or car restoration. Boats won, since Peter's local sailing club at Bosham had a keen fleet of classic dinghies, which could possibly help support a small restoration business.

Having enjoyed a few short courses at the Boat Building Academy in Lyme Regis, Peter spent a "marvellous year" at the International Boat Building Training College in Lowestoft. The first project was to build his own mallet and plane, working without power tools while learning the traditional skills of wood joinery. Peter set up Broadside Boatyard with a fellow student in 2004, but now operates independently. Since then he has worked on a huge range of boats, mostly through word of mouth, ranging from Mirrors and 12 foot Tideways to "doing wooden bits" such as teak cappings on glassfibre yachts. Most jobs

Peter works out of slightly dilapidated, but charming premises, a world away from his abandoned desk in London. The red dinghy is his own Chichester Harbour 18, built in nearby Bosham in 1929.

Jeremy Evans

involve refurbishment and repairs, but totally rebuilding a 12 foot clinker dinghy from Seaview took the best part of a year.

Peter rates the best things about his new work as, "Being active and on my feet all day, no more back pain from sitting at a desk, spending a lot of time outside and breathing life into old boats," which is clearly a passion, particularly when they traditionally built of solid wood

"Being active and on my feet all day, spending a lot of time outside and breathing life into old boats"

and nails. The worst thing is, "Having no money!" While there is plenty of potential work, getting people to pay for old boats is not easy. Furthermore, Peter warns that suitable premises are always likely to be expensive near the water.

If anyone hears the call of a new life in boat restoration, Peter suggests looking very carefully at what colleges offer and making sure it is as close as possible to what you need. Peter recommends the American magazine WoodenBoat *(www.woodenboat.com)* as an excellent source of information, particularly on the wide choice of traditional boatbuilding colleges in the USA. ❖

BOATBUILDING COLLEGES & COURSES

BoatBuilding Academy

The BBA at Lyme Regis is a not-for-profit organisation teaching boatbuilding that can be practical, professional or purely for pleasure. Training courses vary in length from 1 day to 38 weeks.

■ www.boatbuildingacademy.com

City & Guilds 2451

Boatbuilding, Maintenance and Support (2451) is a Vocational Level 2 and 3 course aimed at candidates who wish for career progression within the boat building industry or wish to develop skills and knowledge. Students can expect to gain a thorough knowledge of yacht and boat construction, including assembly and subassembly, hull construction, installation and fitting out, and marine propulsion systems. Many candidates will build a complete boat as part of their course studies.

■ www.cityandguilds.com

International Boat Building Training College

The IBTC is a fee-paying college which claims to provide the widest range of boatbuilding training in the world. At least 24 craft of varying designs and construction, ranging from large seagoing yachts to small dinghies, are being worked on as training projects at any one time. The 47-week Practical Boatbuilding course leads to an IBTC Diploma and the option of City & Guilds 2451 Levels 2/ 3, with Small Boatbuilding, Woodworking Skills, Glass Reinforced Plastics, Knots & Splicing, Basic Boat Plumbing & Electrics, Lofting and Caulking all available as separate courses.

■ www.ibtc.co.uk

CoVE for Marine Industries

CoVE (Centre of Vocational Excellence) for Marine Industries links four training providers across Hampshire and the Isle of Wight, and provides specialist marine training provision for individuals and employers. They offer more than 50 different courses, ranging from 2D CAD for Boat Design to Yacht Maintenance.

■ www.cove4marineindustries.co.uk

Falmouth Marine School

Cornwall's College of the Ocean is a specialist marine college for boatbuilding, marine engineering, marine science, leisure & watersports, and university courses. Courses on offer include Traditional Boatbuilding, Introduction to Boatbuilding Techniques NVQ1, Boatbuilding Techniques NVQ2, Boatbuilding & Maintenance NVQ3.

■ www.cornwall.ac.uk/falmouth

MITEC

Pembrokeshire College's Marine Centre (MITEC) provides a range of courses from beginner to degree level, covering the design and building of marine craft, marine engineering and crewing or skippering boats. MITEC was purpose-built in 2000 with an extensive range of boat building and marine engineerig equipment supported by computer and classroom facilities.

■ www.pembrokeshire.ac/uk/mitec

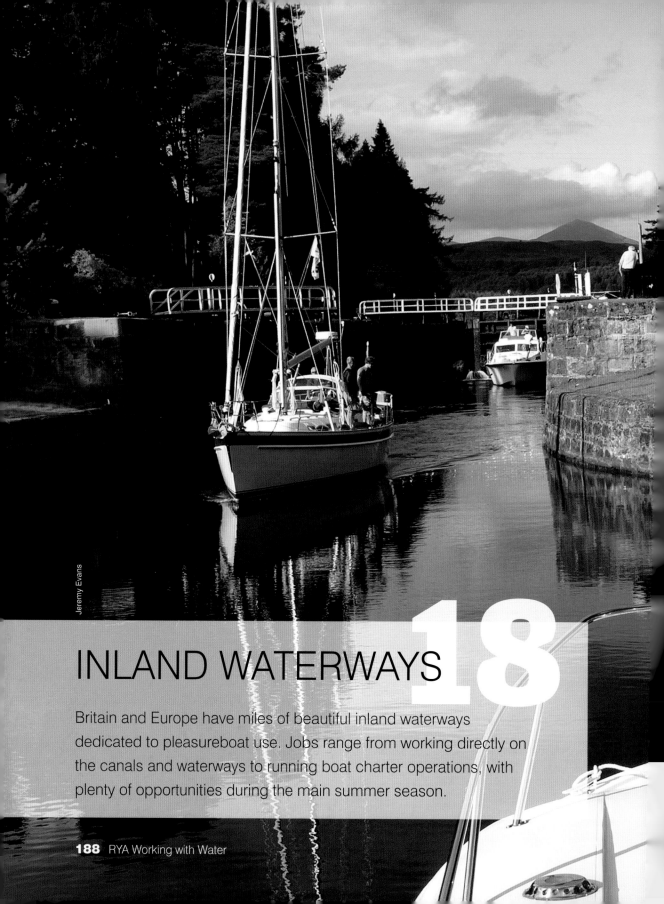

Jeremy Evans

INLAND WATERWAYS 18

Britain and Europe have miles of beautiful inland waterways
dedicated to pleasureboat use. Jobs range from working directly on
the canals and waterways to running boat charter operations, with
plenty of opportunities during the main summer season.

LOCK KEEPER

Mairearaid MacDonell works as Sea Lock Keeper for the west end of the Caledonian Canal in Scotland.

All in a day's work – Mairearaid MacDonell greets a new client on the canal.

Seasonal or full time…

I joined British Waterways as a seasonal lock keeper in March 2001and worked for three seasons, before becoming full time. A total of 38 lock keepers are employed during our busy period from March to October, including 22 seasonal workers, 10 full timers and 6 split role who work with the canal maintenance team from November to March when we catch up with all our pressure washing and maintenance jobs.

The majority of our seasonal staff returns each year. Seasonal workers are given training in Boatmanship Level 1 and full timers in Boatmanship Level 2. All lock keepers are fully trained on locks and bridges before being allowed to work on their own, as well as VHF radio, fire and water safety, first aid, customer service and disability awareness.

Lots of locks…

Working in different locations along the canal can be very different. The Sea Lock where I work is the first port of call for boats wishing to travel west to east. We issue a licence and explain the locking procedure to first time skippers and crew. Any boat needing fuel is bunkered in the basin before setting off through the double lock towards Neptune's Staircase (Banavie Locks) where the fun begins! In contrast to the single locks and swinging bridges further along the canal, it takes 1 hour 30 minutes to get a boat from the bottom to the top of Neptune's Staircase. In the summer, the lock keepers can walk over 10 miles up and down the flight of eight locks.

Best and worst…

One of the best things about being a lock keeper is meeting old and new customers, some of whom have been transiting the canal for over 30 years. One of the worst things is seeing a boat that has come through for many years leaving the canal for the last time, when the owner is retiring from sailing.

The lock keeper's cottage…

There are a few lock keepers living in British Waterways houses, but the majority of old lock houses along the canal are sold or rented out. All lock keepers are informed of vacancies within the British Waterways network. I know of only two people who moved south for work – it's usually the other way round.   ❖

Anyone wishing to be a lock keeper must firstly enjoy dealing with people, secondly have plenty of common sense and thirdly be able to cope under pressure.

CHARTER OPERATOR

After retiring from the army, Ray Norris found a job with a boat hire company based on the Caledonian Canal at Inverness. He eventually set up his own boat hire company, then sold it and established West Highland Sailing & Cruisers in 1980, running a fleet of sailing yachts and motor cruisers from a base at Laggan Locks in the western part of the Caledonian Canal. In restrospect, he says he just "blundered" into what appears to be a fine working liftestyle, but one that can also provide stress and pressure at busy times of the year.

Ray, can you explain what sort of work West Highland Sailing does and how many people you employ?

Basically, we prepare and maintain a fleet of hire boats and instruct customers in their use. We employ five people full time including an office administrator, engineer and housekeeper for all the boats. We also employ numerous part time people depending on our workload and the time of year, including a few who may work two or three days in the winter before going full time during the main season from April through to October.

Enjoying the canal on board a West Highland Cruiser.

Jeremy Evans

What kind of jobs are available?

Preparing the boats for service, instructing customers on how to handle them and ensure they feel confident, fixing anything that goes wrong and cleaning the boats inside and out. There are constant changeovers of boats and customers, so there is always plenty of work. In winter there is a lot of maintenance work and mechanical overhauls, plus comprehensive housekeeping such as removing and cleaning all fabrics. The work goes on, but the hours are shorter.

What qualifications or experience are required?

You simply need the experience to do the job. I get lots of people who tell me they can sail a boat or handle a motor cruiser, but when I say, "Can you mend an engine?" the true answer is frequently "No". If you are keen to work on the inland waterways, I would recommend getting mechanically qualified to work on engines and other parts of a boat. That way you should get the best salary – although don't expect to earn loads of money.

What are the best things and worst things about working on the canal?

The worst is probably having to work for me, possibly long hours and having to be out in some unpleasant weather. The best is working in a very nice environment with beautiful surroundings, as well as meeting people who are on holiday and tend to be relaxed and happy.

■ www.westhighlandsailing.com ❖

I would recommend getting mechanically qualified to work on engines. That way you should get the best salary…

INSTRUCTOR

Willie Arnold set up Avon Boat Courses to help customers develop boat handling and navigational skills on inland waterways.

Willie teaches clients with his own boat on the River Avon.

Getting started…

Setting up a training centre seemed like a good idea, thanks to a lifelong interest in boats and my own mooring on the River Avon. To become an RYA instructor and tester of the ICC Certificate (International Certificate of Competence for Inland Waterways) and CEVNI (European Code for Inland Waterways), I completed the Powerboat Level 2 course at an RYA training centre in North Wales, the Inland Waterways Helmsman course on the canal at Stourport and on the River Severn, and was examined on the River Thames. This complemented my own experience, which started as a child on the Norfolk Broads.

Teaching clients…

When teaching novices, the most important thing is to give them confidence to attempt to handle their boat without too much stress. The key is to go slowly, so when you inevitably hit something, nothing will get damaged!

Enabling novices to realise the fun of boating is one of the greatest pleasures of being an instructor. The greater your experience, the more you will be able to empathise. Safety afloat is paramount. There can be only one captain, so it is important to establish that the person at the helm makes the decisions. This is a good way of giving children real responsibility. I expect children as young as six years old to join in and try everything when I am teaching their parents. This helps ensure that boating is a true family activity and that good, safe practice is established from the start.

Making a living…

Avon Boat Courses is mainly run as a hobby, so makes little more than enough to cover costs which can be quite high, especially insurance for the school. Running a course requires total commitment. It is very hard work as I try to provide real value for money. Tact is also necessary, especially when children turn out to be more competent than their parents.

■ www.avonboatcourses.co.uk   ❖

INLAND WATERWAYS HELMSMAN INSTRUCTOR

In order to become an Inland Waterways Helmsman Instructor you will need to hold the Inland Waters Helmsman Certificate, First Aid certificate and the VHF/SRC Certificate. Maximum age is 65 and the certificate is valid for 5 years. Cost is £220.00 payable to the RYA with a completed application form.

■ email: training@rya.org.uk · Tel: 023 8060 4188.

Summertime activity at Fort Augustus where a major flight of locks provides year-round work for British Waterways staff. You can check for vacancies on canals and rivers throughout the UK under 'Work For Us' at www.britishwaterways.co.uk/home.

Jeremy Evans

MORE WORK ON WATER

Many beach clubs and activity centres require qualified instructors to manage alternative watersports such as kitesurfing, diving, canoeing, kayaking, wakeboarding or waterskiing…

www.flyozone.com

www.flyozone.com

KITESURFING

The International Kiteboarding Organisation (IKO) administers a five-day instructor-training course. Pre-qualification is required to determine personal ability. Candidates must have completed RYA Powerboat Level 2 and have a water based First Aid qualification such as RYA First Aid or PADI Medic. The British Kitesurfing Association administers instructor qualifications for schools with BKSA recognition, linked to the IKO system.

■ www.ikorg.com
■ www.britishkitesurfingassociation.co.uk

DIVING

Neilson

The British Sub Aqua Club (BSAC) administers an Instructor Foundation Course, Open Water Instructor Course and Advanced Instructor Course. The Professional Association of Diving Instructors (PADI) has headquarters in California, with regional offices in Australia, Canada, Japan, Sweden, Switzerland and the UK. PADI professional certification includes Divemaster with responsibility for a group of divers, Assistant Instructor, Open Water Scuba Instructor, Speciality Instructor, Master Scuba Diver Trainer, IDC Staff Instructor, Master Instructor and Course Director.

■ www.bsac.com ■ www.padi.com

Neilson

CANOEING

The British Canoe Union is the governing body for canoe and kayak sport in the UK. The BCU administers Paddlesport Awards with Level 1, 2 and 3 Certificates in Coaching. Minimum age is 16 years for the Level 1 and 17 years for the Level 2 awards.

■ www.bcu.org.uk

Neilson

WATERSKIING

British Water Ski offers three tiers of instructor qualification. Standard Instructor, Club Coach and Senior Coach licences are complemented by instructor qualifications in each division – for instance Wakeboard Instructor or Barefoot Instructor – all of which are widely accepted overseas. A minimum age of 16 is required to achieve the basic instructor qualification.

■ www.britishwaterski.org.uk

FAST TRACK & INTENSIVE INSTRUCTOR TRAINING

There are many providers of fast track training, offering a huge range of courses for people who want to work on water. Here are just a few of the operators you can choose from based in the UK…

FLAGSHIP SUPERYACHT ACADEMY

Superyacht training specialist that works in partnership with the Royal Navy to use spare RN training capacity. Provides individual and whole crew training, including on-board submersibles and helicopters!

■ www.fsya.co.uk

FLYING FISH

Flying Fish provides a wide range of courses, all the way from dinghy instructor to superyacht crew. They specialise in gap year, career break and other fast-track training from centres including Vassiliki in Greece, Club Dahab in Egypt and Sydney's Middle Harbour Yacht Club. Flying Fish also provides dive traineeship.

■ www.flyingfishonline.com

HAMBLE SCHOOL OF YACHTING

Well established sailing school (see page 112) that runs Instructor Courses and Professional Sail Training, with STCW modules ranging from Basic Safety Week (5 days including Elementary First Aid, Personal Survival Techniques, Fire Prevention & Fire Fighting, Personal Safety & Social Responsibilities) to Proficiency in Medical Care on Board Ship (5 days).

■ www.hamble.co.uk

NEILSON ACADEMY

The Neilson Academy provides intensive training in Dahab, Egypt for RYA Dinghy and Windsurfing Instructors combined with Off-Road Trail Leaders (mountain biking). Optional training is available for PADI diver qualifications and kitesurfing.

■ www.neilson.co.uk

Sunsail

SUNSAIL ACADEMY

The Sunsail Professional Academy aims to train skippers and develop their careers. The 2-year course allows students to gain essential industry qualifications whilst building experience across a range of Sunsail bases, with work as a Flotilla, Club and Bareboat skipper during the summer season.

■ www.sunsail.co.uk

STORMFORCE COACHING

Operating in the UK, Greece and Portugal. Courses are available for all RYA Instructor Training, plus Fast-Track courses for Professional Sports Boat Driver (3 weeks), Dinghy & Keelboat Instructor (6 weeks) and Yachtmaster Offshore (17 weeks).

■ www.stormforce.biz

UKSA

The United Kingdom Sailing Academy was a pioneer of fast track and intensive training. With bases at Cowes on the Isle of Wight and in Australia, the UKSA provides the greatest choice of course options for those who want to pursue professional careers on water, incorporating all essential qualifications. Specialised courses include Marine Hospitality Training and Professional Yacht Engineer.

■ www.uksa.org

INDEX

Page numbers in *italics* refer to illustrations.

NOTES

NOTES